Chuckle With Chuck
By Chuck Houghton

About the cover—*I built the Happy bus, Sunshine painted it for me. It was used at Montabella Schools for kindergarten round up and Mecosta Elementary for Bright Start sign-ups at both schools we would take kids and parents for rides on a regular bus so they would know what to expect. Worked Great.*

Notes

Table of Contents

Notes

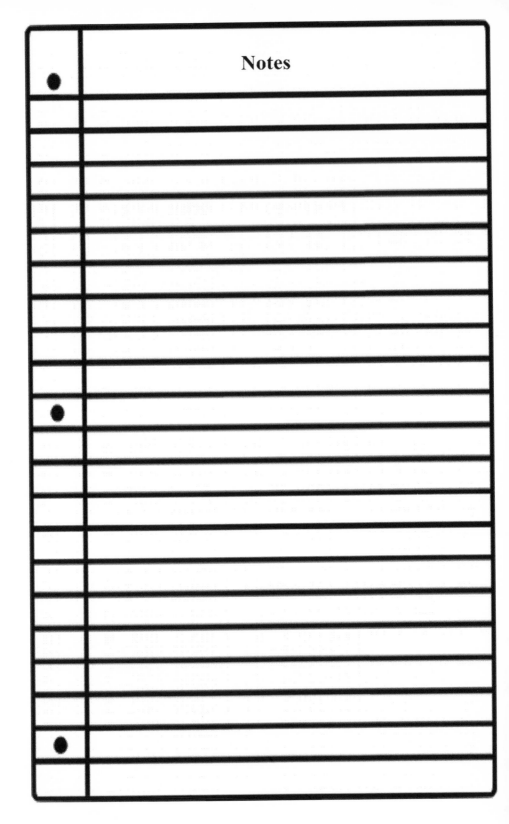

My Desk
My train of memories, thoughts and opinions
engineered by Kathy Nerychel and Shirley Pool.

*My think Tank – the cup my age when I started to write
E.S.P. my mother-in-law cup Extra Special Person
chip out of the cup – rough edged old man – ½ a smile*

Why I Did The Book

Why I did the book is explained. What motivated me. How it energized me. I thank all my memory sources. The people in my writers group: Kathy, Katherine, Joe, Jake, Peggy and Charlene.

As this train of memories, thoughts and opinions starts to move down the tracks, K. our engineer will determine when, where and how often we stop.

I encourage you kids to add your dreams and experiences or fun episodes. That's what the blank pages are for. It's called "family life's circles." Because without you all, there would be no book or reason for one. I had four super great kids and got three more of the same in the best package deal I ever made. Thanks Sunshine.

I hope as you read this something said will trigger a memory, which adds joy to your life. As Mae West said, "Too much of a good thing is wonderful."

I know, I know. Who is Mae West?

Please read on.

Share

Kids, grandkids, friends, please share with me what I remembered of my life. It's all in good fun, what I call common sense mixed with life all wrapped up in one package. As I grow older, life becomes much more enjoyable for me. I muse at the political theater and how accomplished the actors are doing their parts. All trying to prove their way is the only way.

I find much humor in saving ourselves from ourselves. Life, seasoned with age, mellows the music, smooths the speed bumps and even though my eyes are bad, life looks better all the time. What you needed to take care of last week won't spoil for at least another week.

That wonderful woman who shares my everything is now storing it all away. I'm too old to help with people's problems so I create more with my inability to understand, I'm the problem! So with this as a background please review the pages I remember of my life.

To Kathy Nerychel for starting the Tamarack Writers Group

"Why Not?"

Around 10:30 p.m., April 2, I was in a Spectrum Hospital bed with my wife and daughter sitting beside me. I was almost back to "my" normal self from a stroke. The third doctor was checking my reflex, grip, so forth, but she was really there for answers. I'm comfortable being ready for most anything that comes at me. I was totally not ready for her.

"Mr. Houghton, you have many medical problems, and you just had your fourth stroke. Have you thought about suicide?"

I didn't answer immediately. But I can't lie. "Yes, I have."

"How often?"

"Three times."

"Do you have a gun in the house?"

"Yes."

"Mr. Houghton, I can arrange counseling for you if you want it."

"No I don't need it now!"

Doctor: "Why not?"

I looked at the two very silent ladies to my right. My daughter was crying. The look on my wife's face I had never seen before!! I will always feel good about my answer to her, "Why not?" question.

"My daughter has been after me to write a book, ever since she read my yearbook prophesy. It was predicted I would write and publish, "Chuckles with Chuck."

I periodically put articles in the Lakeview paper. Their worker, Kelly, kept after me to go to the Tamarack Writers group. So I did. "Why not?"

Today, I would like to use an analogy for what it's like to come to this weekly meeting. You people are so invigorating and stimulating to my mind. When you write you give a little piece of yourself. Your sharing nurtures me.

Kathy's start of this group is equal to Xmas for me. Your birth of ideas is my growing Xmas tree. All six of you are very unique ornaments on my tree, representing life as you see it, each being memorable and remarkable. You can't be replaced or duplicated. The total brilliance of all your writing lights up my Xmas tree. When your creative genius brings top recommendation, it's Xmas treats time (cake and cookies.) I so much enjoy the look of your success. Xmas comes to me every Thursday at 1 o'clock. If you all give a presentation I get 6 presents per week. So the doctor's "Why not?" is no longer a question. It's a connection to "Why not just keep going?" Thank you all for giving me a purpose. You all deserve cake and cookies.

Notes

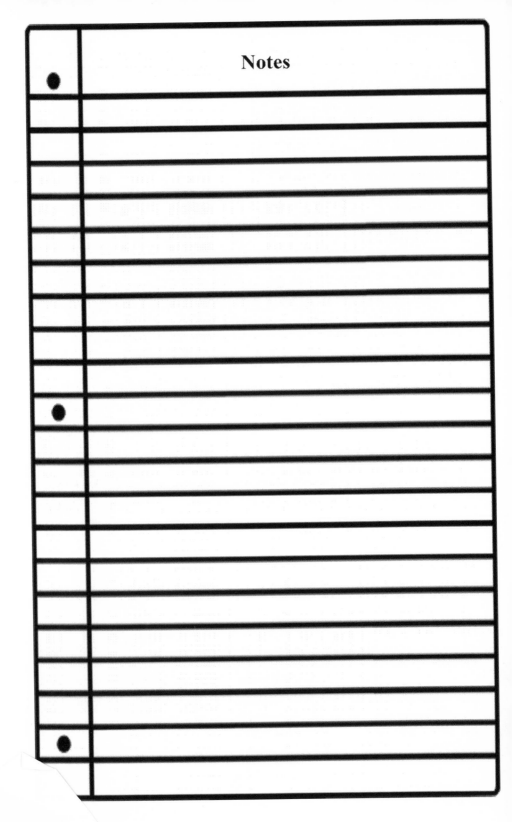

Once Upon A School Bus

Once Upon A School Bus
Introduction:

For 17 wonderful years, I called myself a school bus driver and I want to thank all those parents who had faith in me. When the child enters the bus for the very first time and mom is taking two or three pictures of the procedure, I would always remind mom, "Please be careful of what you say and do from now on, because I will hear all about it."

"We as school bus drivers always wonder what effect or influence we have on kids. Once in a while a kid will give you a great memory. Here are some of mine." **Chuck Houghton**

Once Upon a School Bus...

A short fight ensued in the back of the bus, so I shut my bus down, pulled the key and went back. I said, "Alright, who started this?"

Silence...after a moment one young man stood up, looked me in the eyes, and made my day as he said, "Once you told me that it didn't matter what color I was, if my word was good, I would be a good man, so ....I started it."

Some bus slips are very, very hard to give out. (Chuck said he recently met him in a bank and the man said, "I have never forgotten that bus slip.")

Once Upon a School Bus...

When I stopped driving bus I received some letters from my bus riders. Here is an excerpt from one letter. "You can't quit driving my bus, you gave me my first Bus Slip."

Once Upon a School Bus...

The first thing they said as they entered the bus was, "We went to the cottage for the weekend."

I asked, "Have lots of fun?"

"Yep!" they answered." But I don't think mom and dad did."

I asked, "Why?"

They replied, "Cause they had a hinder-fight Saturday night."

Be careful what you say or do.

Once Upon a School Bus....

A favorite statement by an eighth grade girl, "It was worth a bus slip just to hit him."

Once Upon a School Bus...

The high school art class was outside all afternoon, as I walked out to do my afternoon bus check, they all were gathered around the right side of my bus and were laughing. They stepped aside so I could see the chalk-drawn outline of a human being, partly under my bus with broken arms and legs just like a TV crime scene. They had me dead to right...I loved it!

Once Upon a School Bus....

I did an out of district noon take home run one year. Kids were picked up on the border by their parents. As I pulled up to the running car, the barefoot mom ran through the snow to the bus in a see-through housecoat, grabbed her child and yelled, "Sorry, I overslept." And was gone. No comment.

Once Upon a School Bus...

I was pulling into the high school to drop off the mid-day big kids. I was checking my mirrors when I noticed a brown glob of something sail out of a side window. Checking seat with window, I called out the boy's name and said, "Are you chewing tobacco?"

"No," he answered. "I just spit it out."

"Got ya!" I said.

Once Upon a School Bus...

He was a ward of the state of Michigan because he was picked up after midnight walking the street of a central Michigan town. All alone. He was just four years old as he plunked himself into the front seat of my Head Start bus.

He began yelling and hitting his head, "That's it, that's it. That is why it is called Head Start. It starts here!"

Smart kid!

Once Upon a school Bus...

She was smiling from ear to ear as she climbed the bus steps. I asked, "What's up?"

She answered, "I got $ 5.00 from the Tooth Fairy."

"Wow!" I said, "I only got a quarter from her when I was young." I continued, "How come you got so much?"

"Because," she replied, "My dad said President Clinton gave the Tooth Fairy a raise, so now we get more money."

Once Upon a School Bus...

I was sitting in the bus driver's area, when he walked in. He was about 6'6", full black rough beard, complete motorcycle attire, pointed black leather hat, long black trench coat, high black boots, big belt buckle and a few tattoos. "I'm Mr. _____," he said, with no expression. "Did you give my son a bus slip?"

Slowly I said, "Yes."

He smiled and the room brightened up after he stated, "You have my total support with whatever you need to make him behave on the bus."

"Super Dad," I thought, "My nominee for Father of the Month."

After he left, our mechanic walked in and commented, "We should have him drive bus. We would never have a kid problem."

Once Upon a School Bus...

It was a cool October morning with two high school boys already on the bus. At the second stop two high school girls entered and sat down directly in front of the boys. Even before I had all of my mirrors checked to re-enter M-66, one girl was on her feet with her fist under one boy's nose. I heard the following, "Knock it off you two. My period started this morning and believe me, it's not a good day to mess with me."

Done. Mother Nature wins every time.

Once Upon A School Bus...

It was this Middle Schooler's first year in band. He had that horn with him all of the time; he loved it like a puppy. He would play it quietly behind me on the bus. After the first month, he did not have it any more and was noticeably sad. "Where is your horn?" I asked.

"Gone," he answered. "Mom said she could not afford to rent it any longer."

What I knew was that his chain-smoking mom would not give up her cigarettes so he could have the horn. I never transported a bad kid, but I did meet a few troubled parents.

Once Upon a School Bus...

On our bus everyone was responsible to maintain the bus. As I checked the bus after the afternoon run, I found a cut seat. No one would admit the guilt. After a week, one high school student said two middle school kids had had a dismantled pencil sharpener, but he did not see them do anything. I called the kid's grandpa and appraised him of what I knew about the incident. He said, "I'll get back to you."

About ½ hour later grandpa called back. "How much for a new bus seat cover?"

I answered "$26.00." He said, "Good, they have just about that much in their piggy bank."

As the kids entered the bus the next morning one asked, "How did you catch us?" I just smiled.

Once Upon a School Bus...

I always felt when driving bus you needed to be honest and consistent each and every day. I had an extra run for two years – all big kids. Once, before we left the high school, there was a problem, so I shut the bus down, pulled the key and went to the back of the bus. "Okay, what's up?" I asked.

No answer was heard from anyone. Slowly a rather big young man stood up and looked down on me and said, "I'm not afraid of you!"

"Really," I said. "I'm scared to death of you!"

"Really," he said.

"Yes," I answered.

"Oh," he said, and sat back down. I don't think he believed me.

Once Upon a School Bus…

Same group of big kids, different day. I was waiting to load to go back to the high school. "Oops," problem in the school yard, so I pulled the key and went to investigate. One boy was sitting on the ground with a big welt on the side of his head. "What happened?" I asked.

He said, "I told him he could have a FREE punch."

I laughed, "You're supposed to say you can have the FIRST punch, not a FREE one."

"Oh, okay, I'll get it right the next time." He answered. Then he actually laughed.

I told the kids I trusted them and did everything I could think of to prove it. Kids feel comfortable when they are trusted.

When people talk about driving school bus and I hear statements like "I'd kill them" or "I would be in jail for murder on the first day." When asked, "How can you do it?"

I say, "How can you not do it?"

When a second grader is standing next to your driver's seat with a handful of freshly picked dandelions and says, "These are just for you."

Once Upon a School Bus...

Oops! I think my bus might have a chance of being in the Guinness Book of World Records.

As this story begins, each year, the Michigan State Police completes a safety inspection of all school buses and it was our school's week to be inspected. My bus was used, once a day, by another driver for a single child run. As the driver pulled to a stop behind the bus garage, he was positioned to the left rear of the running police car. This was when bus number 9 made history, by being the only bus to be hit by a police car that was driven by a Michigan State Police bus inspector during bus safety check week and causing property damage.

Footnote: Acknowledging the very high standards and professionalism of our Michigan State Police, it wouldn't surprise me if the officer wrote himself a ticket!

Once Upon a School Bus...
Halloween Story

As I pulled up to his stop, I was laughing. It was Halloween day and this high schooler had gone all out for the occasion. Somewhere he had gotten a fat suit with clothes big enough to cover himself. He was so big he could hardly get in the bus door. The student had to sit in the front seat because he could not get down the aisle. When we got to the high school, he stumbled getting off the bus and fell down.

As we arrived at his home that night, I commented on his artful creation and how much the other kids enjoyed his "get up." I asked how his day had gone and he replied, "It was great and I had a lot of fun." He continued, "I now also have much more compassion for big people than I had just this morning." As he squeezed out the bus door, he fell down again.

I think it is great to have fun and learn something about ourselves at the same time. As my wife regularly tells me, "Chuck, if you didn't learn something today, you just weren't paying attention."

Once Upon a School Bus…

The Superintendent's Ride

I was loading kids for the afternoon take home, when to my surprise the superintendent of schools appeared at my bus door. He stated, "I want to ride your bus this afternoon."

I asked, "Is there something wrong?"

He answered, "I just decided I would ride a few buses to see what it is like."

He got on and sat down in the front seat with a third grader. I introduced them and what followed was an experience of a lifetime for both the superintendent and me. The third grader proceeded to inform us that his father had been an avid drug user. He had overdosed, and was saved in a hospital emergency room. He said, "My dad is making sure none of his kids would ever be a user of drugs."

After the lengthy testimonial concluded, there were a few moments of silence. "Well sir, that was definitely a first for me. I said,

"Me too," the superintendent replied. We both felt the father was doing a great job with his children! However, I never heard of the superintendent riding another bus.

Once Upon a School Bus…

Why bus drivers check around their bus!

While loading and unloading elementary students, I noticed one kid crawling under my bus behind my left dual tires. Later that summer I ended up playing a round of golf with the child's parents. Part way through the round they discovered that we had a common denominator. They said their child would never, ever do that trick again. They said their child would never forget what I had said to him. But I have totally forgotten what I did say.

The story above happened when I took elementary students from our school to another school. The child under the bus was from the other school.

Once Upon a School Bus….
Grandparents

Grandparents are a very special group of people. When things aren't normal for parents, you are dealing with grandparents who are filling in for mom and dad. As a bus driver, I truly believe grandparents are on earth to fill in for angels and saints, who need a day off. I was eating lunch when a granddad walked up to my table. He asked if I had a minute. "Sure," I said, "Sit down."

He said, "You drive my grandson's bus, so I'm checking in with you." He continued, "My grandson is very overweight and timid. Could you make sure no one teases or bullies him?"

I replied, "You can rest assured that will not happen on my bus." I continued, "Can you remember years ago when we rode the same bus, I was teased about being fat?"

"No," he said, "I don't." (Funny, I thought to myself, you were the one doing the teasing!)

(I never carry grudges.) Gramps was concerned about his grandson and his heart was in the right place and this is what counts with me. Besides we are not born saints, we have to earn it and he was earning it.

Once Upon a School Bus...
Once is Enough

It was about 11:05 on a Tuesday morning as I unloaded the Career Center kids to the Vestaburg bus. I started experiencing a feeling I had never had before, NO PAIN, just weird. I had one more student to drop off behind the Depot gas station in Edmore. I did that, but I knew I shouldn't drive any farther.

I shut the bus down and entered The Depot and asked my friend Skip if he would take me to the clinic. He said, "Yup."

I walked up to the sign in window at the clinic and said, "I think I have a problem."

She looked up at me, stood up and said, "Yes, you do."

In about 15 minutes they told me it was a heart attack-in-progress. Paul Clouse, PA, called my wife, who was in Grand Rapids, and told her to stay there, because I would be soon going there by helicopter. He then notified the ambulance to get me to the Sheridan Hospital, and he called the bus garage to pick up the bus keys. Those people were great!

Joe the EMT in the ambulance told me later he had to treat me twice from Edmore to Sheridan. "Thanks, Joe!" As they carried me in the Sheridan ER waiting for the helicopter, one of the reasons you drive bus happened. I opened my eyes and standing at the foot of my bed was one of my Career Center kids. Her hand was covering her mouth. She never said a word, but I will never forget the look in her eyes. She still did not move and I said to her, "It's all right, Hon, I'm not dying today."

It seemed like I went right from the helicopter to the operating room, simultaneously a nurse said to me, "Mr. Houghton, you are now going to sleep and when you wake up, you will be all FIXED."

I told her, "I got FIXED when I was 27." I went to sleep to the sound of laughter!

Note: To explain how good and efficient the medical people are in the state of Michigan, from the time the feeling started at the bus stop until I woke up in recovery was only 3 hours and 35 minutes. Paul

Clouse, PA recently began work for the VA Hospital in Grand Rapids.

Once Upon a School Bus...

Four year old, dark hair shining, brown eyes, 60 pounds of mischief, always smiling, my third stop on my second preschool run of the day. His family lived in the lowest level of a two-story old folks home. Mom worked full time upstairs, and was prone to old people accidents. Mom always escorted him to the bus in the morning. Dad got him off at night. This morning Dad brought him to the bus. The little guy rushed ahead, jumped on my bus, rushed to my side, announced to me, to his dad's total shock, "My mom couldn't bring me to the bus this morning because she was all s____!"

I'm glad I had my seatbelt on, or I would have hit the floor laughing.

Once Upon a School Bus...

I was in my fifties when I started driving bus. Kids sometimes don't know or recognize you when they see you somewhere other than on the bus. At the start of my first year of driving, I was in a grocery store and I noticed a little girl that rode my bus. I waved at her. She looked scared and hid behind her mom. Her mom looked at me very cautiously and I said, "I'm your school bus driver. Don't you remember me?"

She looked at me for a moment and said, "No you're not bald in front."

When I drove Head Start bus, I had a wonderful lady for a bus aide. Of course she and I were always on the bus when the kids rode. One night I was all by myself at a basketball game at a different school, and one of my riders was there with her grandmother. Her grandmother let her walk over to say "hi" to me. Then she said, "Where is your wife?"

Once Upon a School Bus...
Paper Wad Fight on the School Bus-Don't Tell the Super!

There are good reasons for all school bus rules. Children's safety is absolutely the total goal of all transportation systems. The bus ride home on the last day of school was always a celebration to be celebrated. A paper wad fight on a moving bus is not acceptable under any conditions. But a planned paper wad fight on a stationary bus is do-able.

As the kids entered the bus for the year-end last ride home, each received a full sheet of soft paper. "On my command, wad up your paper and begin. The paper fight will last five minutes, stop on my order, then we will *all* clean up the paper wads. Make all the noise you want, put up all the windows. Nothing leaves the bus. I have three sheets of paper and I think most of you can't hit the inside of a bus! Start now!"

P.S. Boy, did they prove me wrong! When we stopped 75% of the wads were in the left front of the bus.

Once Upon a School Bus...
Thank you

Well readers, this is my last stop. I really enjoyed having you all on board bus 9. I hope sharing some of my experiences will bring a smile and a positive thought to you every time one of those big yellow buses comes into view. No vehicle carries a more valuable cargo, so please give them all the space they need and always wave at the driver. But most importantly, WATCH OUT FOR THE KIDS. You never know what they might do.

And thank you, *Lakeview Area News* for printing my memories and Shirley Pool for editing them.

Notes

Around the World with Chuck

**England...Italy...Sicily...Vatican...India...Thailand...
Singapore...Taiwan...Hong Kong...Guam...Mexico
Hawaii**

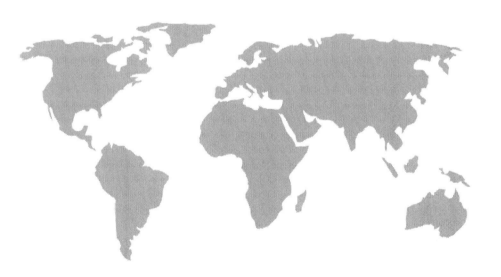

Part 1 of a Multi-Part Series
Edited by Shirley Pool

You may remember this past year that Charles "Chuck" Houghton shared some of his mostly humorous school bus driving stories. He asked if I would once again assist him with his memories from an around-the-world trip he took through the Kellogg Farmers Study Program. The program was initiated by Michigan State University in the fall of 1965. There were four study groups and a total of 120 participants. Chuck was in the fourth group, which began in 1968 and lasted over a three-year period. Part of the study took place in Michigan, but the final year they traveled to other countries. The two main objectives were to build a better understanding of the economic, political, and social framework of our society and to use this framework to analyze the complex problems facing agriculture and rural communities.

While reading the stories, Chuck wants you to understand that they took place over 40 years ago and no doubt some changes have taken place. Houghton also enjoys remembering the humorous side of life, and in no way intends to judge or make fun of anyone. Chuck noted that he was able to see many of the beautiful tourist attractions, but instead wishes to talk about the more common way of life in the countries he visited...the things that you do not see on television.

The trip begins.

We left Detroit six hours late because our airplane had a water contamination problem. It was 1971 and at the time, people were hijacking airplanes, so we had undercover police on board. There were about 50 people flying to London, England and 32 were farmers.

I struck up a conversation with a 25-year-old fellow and said, "You look like a sky Dick to me. Are you?"

He laughed and replied, "I wish I was. My rich uncle told me that if I would finish college with a degree, he would pay for an around the world trip."

He continued, "I did it, and I am making the trip."

I congratulated him. It was now about 2 a.m. and I had been up about 21 hours. I was tired and went to sleep, and woke up about 5 a.m. When I stood up a fellow farmer yelled at me. He had been talking to the same 25-year-old and said, "Chuck, you were right, he is an airline cop!"

As I joined the two, the officer handed me his gun, which surprised me. I said, "How do you know I won't hijack this plane?

The cop laughed and replied, "First, we weren't worried very much about 32 farmers. Second, the gun isn't loaded and third, my partner is standing right behind you and *his* gun is loaded."

I gave the gun back and turned around. His partner was a middle-aged, silver-haired gentleman with a great smile. He said to me, "Not only is my gun loaded, but also I must be able to hit a 50 cent piece at 50 feet...and I can."

With that statement, my around the world trip really began.

We landed in London and we needed to transfer for the flight to Italy. We had to leave one area and cross streets to our departure terminal. London fog is terrible and if you have long arms, you can't see your fingers. As I was about to cross the first street, I heard nothing from my left, only from my right, so I thought I was safe until halfway across the street. WRONG! My first step was almost fatal because in London they drive on the wrong side of the street.

Part Two

From London to Rome we flew over the Alps. It was a very cloudy day. While flying above them, the mountain peaks looked like inverted icicles as they protruded through the clouds. They were unbelievably beautiful and sparkled like diamonds in the sunshine.

We landed in Rome, picked up our bags, found our bus and headed for our hotel. At the first stoplight two people were frantically pounding on the outside of our bus. It seems that no one did a head count at the airport and we left two farmers behind!

They did not speak Italian or know the name of the hotel and literally had to run the bus down or be lost in Rome. You have to admit it was pretty funny to see two screaming Americans chasing a bus down a street in Rome.

The history in Italy and Sicily is beyond describing, so I am just going to share some observations and experiences I had while there in 1971.

1. You could buy fresh oysters on most street corners.
2. I never had a good slice of pizza the entire time I was there.
3. Octopus looked and tasted like half-cooked egg white with a rubber texture.
4. In Sicily we had lunch with members of the Mafia and at the time they were respected as much, if not more, than the police.
5. We visited one Catholic Church and the entire ceiling was made of sold gold. There were no photos allowed.
6. Because we were late, our plane from Sicily to Rome was way behind schedule, but they waited for us. A male flight attendant grabbed me by the arm and said with a big grin, "Get your ruddy butt in that seat," and we were off to India.

7. As we came in to land in India, the entire area was totally flat. It was a clear day, but just off the end of the runway there were three totally crashed passenger jet planes.

8. During the trip to India I visited with a very wealthy Indian who talked me into trying some of the flight cuisine. BAD IDEA! I was sick with diarrhea all the night as well as the next day. A fellow farmer gave me two calf pills for diarrhea, which were as big as my little finger, but they saved me.

Part 3

I am not being critical of the way people lived in these countries. One of the reasons for this trip was education to actually see and experience it. Let's talk about India in the early 1970's. We were in India twice as long as anywhere else.

1. Unless we were in a major city, most public bathrooms were a wooden fence built in a square with some partitions, dirt floor, no roof, no seats, no urinals, and no paper. Bring your own grass!

2. In the first hotel I stayed in, the water coming out of the faucets was green!

3. Cashews were two times bigger than in the U.S.
4. Cows walked through the streets just about everywhere and people fed them. While the cow ate, the people milked it. The milk was fresher than home delivery. The non-dairy farmers had to watch where they stepped.
5. However, even with my dairy background, my tolerance for aroma was severely tested when I had lunch with an open sewer running under the table where I ate.
6. Handicapped and poor people were plentiful, along with many beggars. I will never forget one man who moved by walking on his knuckles and butt because he had no legs.
7. We were invited out to a prominent person's house one evening for dinner. As we toured his home, he was very proud of his many household conveniences. One fellow farmer asked if he had a dishwasher. The homeowner smiled and answered, "Yes, come and I will show you." He led us down a short narrow hall to a shower stall with a front ledge about a foot high with a seat on the back wall. One of his servants was sitting on the seat with his bare feet in about six inches of gray water washing our dishes!

8. We were in both Delhi and Bombay and from those two cities we took bus trips to visit many temples, shrines, etc. Again I reiterate there were many, many beautiful religious and historical things to see. I visited Saint Thomas' Tomb in India, but this story is more about the trip and my experiences…the little things you never forget!

9. When we traveled out of the city, it was usually a one-lane blacktop road, no side roads, just dirt paths. It was grain harvest season and grain was spread on the blacktop to dry. Our bus driver drove through the grain, NOT around it, so most of it was blown back into the dirt, a loss for its owner, who came screaming out of his hut. The bus driver instantly became very unpopular with us.

Part 4

Before I continue with my trip, I think I need to explain some of the fine details about our travel. We had to hand-wash our own laundry during our trip around the world. We were instructed to bring a spring coat, two shirts, two pairs of pants, SILK UNDERWEAR, and boy did I dislike that…It felt like I had ants in my pants! We were also told to bring many pairs of socks! Why? Because when we entered all of the temples, we had to remove our shoes, but the cows, cats, and dogs didn't. Needless to say, we threw away many socks!

O.K. back to the trip: On one trip we left the black top and traveled on a dirt road being constructed and stopped when we got to the workers who were building the road. We were surprised to see about 125 women with wheelbarrows, shovels, picks, and hoes doing the work. Granted the land had no trees and it was flat...But they were it! We stepped off of the bus and one of our guys had a Polaroid camera. He took a picture of two of the workers and then gave it to them. That's when the fun began. The two women started jumping up and down and yelling.

All of the workers dropped their tools and got in a group to get their picture taken. The male supervisors had a fit, but they were out-numbered by about 125 to 3. After the photos were taken, the ladies all went back to work. They only made a dollar a day.

On that same trip, we visited a school in a rural village. It was a wooden structure and the entire school consisted of one room. It was about 8x10 feet with two windows. However, there was no glass in the windows and no door, only an opening where the door should have been. There were no books, paper or pencils, only a small chalkboard with chalk.

While we were in India, I was the only farmer to become infected with malaria. It didn't get bad until the last week of the trip. The way malaria affected me was that about every 12 hours I would have a really bad migraine headache that would last for about an hour and a half. Half of that time I would be burning up, and the other half, I would freeze.

Part 5

On the long ride out to the Taj Mahal, the bus drove on a single black top road and offered no bathrooms...period! Our driver stopped by a village, and after we had relieved ourselves, the driver asked if we would like a 'Coke.' Boy did that sound GREAT. There were very few liquids we could drink and feel safe. He then opened the engine compartment in the back of the bus and treated us all to a 100 degree-plus HOT Coke.

The Taj Mahal is definitely one of the Seven Wonders of the World. It is beautiful! The four corners slant out so if there is an earthquake, they will not fall on the tomb. The king had this tomb built for his wife. After it was built, the king cut off the hands of the builder and blinded him, so that he could not build anything prettier. What a thank you for a job well done!

It was very dark for the long ride back to town and the driver did not turn on his headlights. We were all very nervous about riding in the dark with no lights. All of a sudden the bus came to a screeching stop and the driver turned on his lights. We were looking straight in the eyes of a full-sized elephant!

We had a private meeting with the president of India. I don't remember why, but it was very important to our group because the Michigan State University professor, who was responsible for our total trip, received a personal autographed book written by the president of India.

Part 6

We left India on a 737 to go to Thailand. My roomie for the trip had a pilot's license, so he asked if he was allowed in the cabin of the plane. Farmers must be universally trusted because they said, "Yes."

After about an hour he returned to his seat, smiled and said, "It was great!" He told me that I was also cleared to go up to the cabin of the plane. While I was up front, we were flying N-NE over Vietnam. As we approached the DMZ we banked hard to the right and stayed over South Vietnam, because of the war.

One of the first things we did in Thailand was to take a bus trip to visit a M.S.U. graduate, who had a big pig farm. He had all of his pig feed shipped in and he said he made very little profit on his pigs. But he designed his pig lots so it all drained into three big ponds. He would wash all of the pig manure into the ponds. He was getting rich selling poop-fed fish to local businesses! We did not eat any fish.

On that same day we went to the pig farm, there were two ladies from New York City, New York. As we soon found out, they were both newly retired chemical engineers. One lady slowly made her way through the group to the back of the bus where I was sitting. "Where in Michigan do you live?" she inquired.

"Blanchard," I replied.

"Is there a Millbrook?" she asked.

"Actually, there is an East and a West Millbrook," I answered.

"I was born there," she added.

Now this is where the story gets even better. She asked, "Do you know of any people named Broomfield?"

I answered, "We have a Bill Broomfield living in our tenant house." It turned out that he was her first cousin. Just imagine meeting her 12,000 miles from home. SMALL WORLD!

Part 7

One evening while in Bangkok, Thailand, two of the guys in our group noticed a good American western was playing at a movie theater so they went to see the show. It was a big laugh to see an American movie because is was in Thai and not English. I could only guess what "Howdy, Ma'am," sounded like in the Thai language. Ha, ha!

Bangkok used rickshaws for transportation to get around the city. Two of our biggest farmers paid for a short ride in one. It just happened that the first 30 feet or so was downhill and the rickshaw puller was a small man who only weighed about 125 pounds. As the puller picked up the wooden shafts, the two men leaned back in their seat and the weight of the men picked the small man's feet up off from the ground. The 30 feet were covered in about seven seconds, along with much yelling and #$%^&& by the driver. At the bottom of the hill, the farmers leaned forward, the puller's feet hit the ground, and the ride was over.

One thing I remember about Taiwan was our guide stated that there was NO crime there because the punishment for all crime was death, and that was in 1971.

Landing in Hong Kong Airport on their one and only runway was truly memorable. The runway was not as wide as the length of the wingspan of the plane. At the end of the runway stood mountains. At night they would work on making the runway longer by dumping fill-dirt into the ocean. This would take place after midnight.

By the time I got to Hawaii, I was very sick with malaria, however I do remember standing three feet from molten lava that was red hot and was covering the road.

I learned that there is a flower that only grows in old volcanoes and nowhere else in the entire world. So where does it come from?

Pearl Harbor is a must see for everyone. Michigan is still the best place in the world to live!

Part 8

Please allow me to tell you a little about how the Kellogg Farmer Program worked. We would meet in Lansing at the Kellogg Center on the MSU Campus for a week at a time, many times during the winter. We were exposed to the opera, ballet, musicals, symphony, orchestras and plays as well as the normal educational subjects. The thing that made the experiences so great was that before we attended these events, the professor would tell us what to look for, or a piece of history about a play we were about to see. We went to see Death of a Salesman and others like it. Another interesting piece of knowledge is that musicians take their instruments apart during a concert to clean the moisture from them and then put them back together again during a song.

Almost all of our group was MSU grads. I didn't go to college. So many of the guys knew the profs who came to talk. One morning class was about half over, when one of our group, who had played poker late the night before, took off his shoes, leaned his chair up against the wall, put his feet on the table and quickly went to sleep. The prof never stopped talking, but picked up his information, rolled it into a very tight ball, continued talking and slowly walked down the center of the U shaped tables, where we all were sitting. When he got to the sleeping farmer, he took his newly created paper club and hit the farmer on the bottom of his sock-covered feet. It was as loud as a gunshot.

The prof had to stop talking because he was drowned out by 29 laughing farmers. I know the prof enjoyed it as much as we did.

The lesson: Show no respect, receive no respect!

Part 9

I was a Kellogg Farmer the year of the Detroit riot and as part of one week's classes we spent two days in Detroit. We were divided into groups of three or four along with one person who was engaged in a Detroit business. We farmers had a V.P. from Detroit Edison as our leader. We toured the devastated areas with some black community leaders. The most interesting point made was the fact that not all building or businesses in a block were destroyed. We were told that good and honest businesses were left alone, and the rest were damaged or burned!

Our V.P. was a member of the "New Detroit Committee" and their goal was to rebuild the city. They had a morning meeting so we were invited to attend. We were introduced as representatives of the Kellogg Foundation and were seated separately around a very large table of about 30 people. I was placed next to a very elegantly dressed, middle-aged lady, white gloves and all. She smiled and asked, "Do you work for Kellogg?"

"No, I responded, "I am sponsored by Kellogg."

She then inquired, "If you don't work for Kellogg, what do you do?"

I replied, "I'm a dairy farmer from Blanchard, Michigan."

"Oh," she replied and never spoke another word to me.

I thought to myself, "This group is going to rebuild Detroit?"

Part 10

Our V.P. took us to a Hugh Heffner Playboy Club for lunch. He had two reasons. The first one was because the food was fantastic. The second one I'll have to explain. As we entered the club we were greeted by two beautiful young ladies in the normal Playboy Bunny costumes. Our V.P. knew each one on a first name basis. He said, "Ladies, this is your lucky day because these three gentlemen are farmers from our great state, but more important, the tall one in the group is the largest rabbit producer in Michigan." He continued, "He has generously agreed to sign autographs for all of the ladies working today!"

We had the opportunity to visit a mushroom farm in the Thumb area and it was an interesting process. First, loose clean straw is piled up about 6 feet wide by 8 feet high and 150 feet long. They had a machine that was able to drive and straddle over the top of the pile and fluff the straw with tines, while it sprayed water over it. The water and the fluffing create heat and sterilize the straw. After many treatments the straw is then transferred by hand to another building, which is completely dark. It has rows and rows of bunks just like bunk beds. They were four bunks high and each bunk was about four inches deep. The bunks are filled with the straw and seeded. The building was heated and no lights were used. The mushrooms are picked by hand by pickers wearing lighted hats like miners wear. The year was 1969.

Part 11

The second year we traveled the southern United States. In Georgia we visited a family group of 13 fully grown people who lived in a two-room house. The eight beds completely filled one room. The kitchen and dining room filled the second room. They had no running water, no bathroom, and again I am not judging people, the program was to expose us to life in the United States and world.

We also visited an insane asylum in Georgia. It was a dark and dreary building. In one area the people just sat in chairs and did nothing. We were then taken to a rather large room and a lady performed a ballet for us. After she finished, she left and about 15 minutes later returned and did an imitation of a strip tease dance. She had multiple personalities. The place was very depressing.

We visited some businesses in Texas and then crossed over into Mexico. While we were there, one farmer purchased six small bottles of whiskey and a cowboy hat. He put the whiskey on his head then placed the hat over the whiskey and went through customs undetected. NO charge!

Part 12

One more fun fact, as we waited on the runway for our luggage to be transferred to our plane, one farmer was looking out his window and began laughing. It seems he noticed that a big suitcase had fallen off the baggage cart onto the runway. An incoming jet ran over it and flattened it to about two inches thick. We laughed again when that same farmer was called into the terminal to pick out a new suitcase.

Because of time flying East, two of our group went to Mass two days in a row.

I learned a valuable lesson from a Vietnam Vet. We were discussing how in Vietnam total villages were destroyed by fire. I commented that there wasn't much financial expense to rebuilding a straw hut. The vet said, "Chuck, it has nothing to do with money; they lost their home and everything a home stands for and represents."

Did you have a good time on my trip? It was a great experience for me. Thank you to the Lakeview Area News and Shirley Pool.

Fun Stuff

Turtle and the Hare – The Draw

"Hey, Hare, today is a great day to cross the road. Three cars missed me and I wasn't even moving. They must have flunked driving school. Again, my lucky day. Hare, one driver stopped, picked me up and put me in the pond. Sorry, that will never happen to you."

"How come, rabbit? I bury my kids and wait until they are born. You lug yours around for two months. Who's the smart one on that? We are changing the rules of our next race: It will be a water race. You might want to learn how to "Dog" paddle.

We will never have equal ground to race, so let's play hide and seek. "You're it." I'm already hid.

I would never trade places with you hare, I always have a home to go to. Besides I'm fearless. I don't run away from anything. I can't be beat, Hare, it's "National Turtle Day."

"I concede turtle. You have just won the first *running* your mouth contest. But "just" by a hair!"

Ha ha! I hope you're shell-shocked!

Dog Gone

Five days, no word. Our cocker spaniel-beagle mix, pheasant-hunting, phenomenon was gone. She was last seen following my cousin and I riding our bikes to school, a four-mile trip. About noon my dad's sister stopped in. "I'm very sure I found your dog,"

Auntie hunted with mom and dad so we had hope she did. We stopped beside their cornfield (a mile and a half from home) and were led out into the corn to our dog. "How in the world could you find her here?"

The dog could no longer walk. She had been hit by a vehicle. The answer: Auntie: "For the last three days when I fed our dog his table scraps, he would carry some of his food into the cornfield. Today, I followed him, and he was feeding your dog."

Yes, she lived to hunt again. No, money couldn't buy a dog like him.

Cricket

Good morning, no problems doing chores, been up for 2-1/2 hours, let's eat breakfast. As I removed my barn clothes I also let our hot dog breed of a house dog, Cricket, out to run. She made a bee line for a new cat I hadn't noticed sitting in the yard. The cat didn't move, just sat there. Our pet served notice: CAT GET OUT OF MY YARD!

Nothing. As Cricket circled the cat, it raised its right front leg. It didn't have a paw, only a bone end. The cat was larger than the dog. They were now face to face. Cat still hadn't moved. Cricket charged; with perfect timing the cat leveled Cricket on one strong right front leg to the head. Our dog regained her feet and walked slowly and quietly back to the house.

Watching, I realized new yard rules were now in place. Don't mess with Big Dog is out; the big cat is in!!!

LESSON Folks: Handicapped doesn't necessarily mean vulnerable.

P.S. It was like watching a cartoon.

Howard and the Feather

Early morning. I was staying overnight with my favorite cousin, the closest person to a brother I would ever have. We were awakened by his older brother's snoring. He being of age to date, we weren't.

The sleep time was short, and he was dead to the world. As the ZZZZZZs increased in volume, cuz put his finger to his lips for me to be very quiet. With a feather extracted from his pillow, he approached his brother's bed. As the air was being sucked in, the feather was dropped into the open mouth.

Cuz jumped back into our bed to watch. Coughing, snuffing, sneezing, gagging lasted at least 30 seconds. Cuz couldn't help himself. He laughed. Older brother knew immediately he had been had. The swearing started. Cuz jumped up, out the window, across the porch roof, eight feet to the ground, 300 feet to the barn. No p.j.'s just shorts and T-shirts. Cuz didn't make it. He always said the pounding he got was worth it!

Roxie

Roxie: tall, long-legged, white, beautiful, extra smart, very gentle, marvelous green eyes. One fantastic horse. She was my cousin's animal for 37 years. Almost a family member. Roxie was different from other horses in one very special way. She determined her ground speed by the size of her rider. The larger the rider, the faster she would run. It was not taught. It was something she did. No one was able to explain why. Or change it. Or wanted to.

My cousin Jack, Roxie's owner, did win many races, but he was the only one who could make it happen. Truly a one-man horse.

Smoke!

Driving home from work, approaching my driveway, I saw smoke coming out of the open porch door. I rushed into a house full of smoke. I could just see mom taking a pie out of the oven. It was put in to bake without unwrapping it.

The smoke alarm lay broken on the floor. My mom said to me, "You have to put that fire alarm closer to the floor. I had to beat it off the wall with my cane!"

Hummingbirds

Being a caregiver, caring for mom, was a great job. At 90 plus, she couldn't drive, needed help with most things, eyesight not great, but kept busy with her hobbies. I purchased a hummingbird feeder so mom could watch and enjoy the birds.

Uncle Clyde came at least once a week to play euchre. First visit after the feeder was up, mom was all excited. "Clyde, I had 15 different hummingbirds come to the feeder today!"

"All at once?" he asked.

"Oh no," she answered, "one at a time."

Clyde just smiled and never said a word.

Rubbery Knees Optometrist

At 94, Mom made many visits to her optometrist for cataract removal. As he performed many tests on her, much conversation occurred between them. Somehow exercise was discussed. Mom surprised the optometrist saying, "Oh yes, I exercise 15 minutes every day."

He turned to me with a puzzled look on his face. I didn't know what she was talking about. "You exercise every day?" he asked.

"Oh yes, I rub my knees 15 minutes every day!"

Mailman

Dick Merrill was our mailman for a century. He was in our lives in many ways: bowling, golf partner, friend.

When he first started, people left him notes. He would take care of it. No phone, but you always had Dick. Long after retirement Dick became ill. I was able to visit him and talk. He would reminisce about his job. Once one of my mother's presents, he had received was brought up. (A piece of pie.)

I knew mom didn't like to take the time it took to cook, but she was a generous person. As Dick remembered, mom knew he might not like it, so along with the piece of pie came a poem he loved:

Dick
If the going seems rough
When you bite this crust
Don't give it another try.
Just open the window, I suggest, and let the whole thing fly.
Peg Houghton

What You See Is What You Get!

As life cycles, entering my second childhood is far more enjoyable than I imagined it would be. Simple tasks, like opening a door or picking up something I just dropped. People rush to your aid and they always smile when they do. They feel good for doing it. You feel better because you didn't have to. Two warm feelings are better than one. A kid would think like that.

Wednesday, I was about to enter a Dollar Store. I dropped my tablet. The store door opened and a lady scooped up my dropped item and held the door. I thanked her then commented, "Given a choice, I think I would rather look old instead of growing old."

"That's something," she replied, "I would have to think about."

I guess it's which side of the "vanity" you like.

* * * * *

We start as a twinkle in your daddy's eye. If you do good, you end as a tear in your children's eyes.

Got Ya!!
You can tell when you're really old. I only do what I want to do. I never do what I DON'T want to do. One reason is, I can't.
The other is, I can't remember how.

Besides, I'm too busy getting out of everyone's road. I have organized doing nothing to the point where no one can tell how good I'm at it. But it's really hard to do. I set and think about nothing all the time.

Life is passing you by when your spouse dusts your favorite chair while you're still in it!

When your "Can do" can't keep up with your "Want to."

When you get a muscle cramp applying underarm deodorant.

Growing old isn't bad if you can't remember what you're missing. So if you've got time to read this, how old are you?

Cheers

Solving problems with no hard feelings is a true art, but most of the time it's just luck. Dealing with one under the influence, each time, is different. I was attending a very large graduation party. Carrying my food, I located a place to sit. About halfway through my meal the other side of the table cleared. Soon it refilled with a group of drinkers. Not food, just drink. Very soon the physically big man across the table from me had too much and was drinking more and started using bad language. I asked him to correct his use of words. He leaned closer to me and said, "There are no kids close to us, I'll talk anyway I want."

I leaned closer to him and answered, "That old man you're looking at is in his second childhood and doesn't need to hear you. So please stop.!"

I received a surprised look, then a laugh. His reply, "You got me gramps."

He never said another bad word. Amen.

Old Men Marrying Young Women and Starting a Family

1. Not many businesses offer both childcare and adult care as a package deal.
2. Must find a school with a ramp.
3. Dad and baby can eat the same food; buy in bulk.
4. Won't have any problem, deciding who gets which size bib.
5. Both will need diapers.
6. Will need rails on all beds.
7. If you're lucky, you'll only need one potty chair. If not, write "dad" on the big one.
8. The state decides who sits in the front car seat.
9. The wife soon learns the husband came pre-spoiled. She will need to do the child herself.
10. Should buy a child size stationary bike, so the kid can exercise with dad. Most likely mom will need to explain to dad why it's not possible to coast on a stationary bike.
11. Must have a split screen TV for kids' programs and sports.
12. If mom is lucky, dad will be partly deaf, so one baby won't wake up the other.

13.   As time goes by, mom will tell one, "No you can't do it." The other she will need to explain why it's not possible.

14.   The color of one's hair will help determine the difference between childhood and second childhood. Plus there will be a difference in the kind of bottle each wants.

What's In a Name?

By Charles Frederick Houghton

I have been called Chuck, Charlie, Chuckie Fred, Chuckles, Chuckie Cheese, Up Chuck, Charlester, Chuck it, Sir Charles, and Chuckie. If a 6'6" 350 pound man calls you "Chuckie" the name is immediately acceptable. Plus you smile and say, "Yes, sir."

When I was young and heard "Charles Frederick" being summoned I automatically knew my name just changed to "mud." I'm looking for a place to hide.

So folks, what's in a name? Honestly there's nothing until you back it up by being a person of high standards for oneself and for others. The same goes for long running business.

Save

Learning to save is a very important part of life. Of course people stockpile many things besides money: buttons, earrings, license plates, key chains, antiques, junk. How about wisdom? Making friends is much harder than impressing people. But it's worth 100 times more. This I suppose is debatable. But I think to really know someone is better than "who you know."

Personal internal wealth beats picket book wealth every time. Do you enjoy blowing your horn and waving at the ragged-dressed old man on the rusty old bike, picking up cans along the road? If so, you are on your way to a personally richer life. The wealthiest people don't count their money. They count their positive relationships.

Taking a supper hour break from a school bus drivers meeting in Grand Rapids, Michigan I met a street person beside the Gerald R. Ford Museum. He was settled in for the night. Our conversation soon led to why a college grad was living on the street.

Not broke – 25 years of age, physically fit, very articulate. Why this? At the time I thought he was nuts! Now I think he was wise. He rationale: "How could I know I would make it all the way, if I didn't start at the bottom!"

Rich with wisdom!

Tree of Life

Once in a while I hear of or get to witness something so good it takes the wrinkles out of the old heart. Saturday night was the Isabella County Fair 4H Auction of the Kid's projects. I was there for my granddaughter's table sale. The kids get all the money from the sale. Each kid stands on stage, a flat bed wagon, while their creation sells.

Item Number 124 was an 8" high tree made from copper wire with a story and a goal. The young man was not keeping the sale money. He was an active member of a fundraiser for two family members with cancer. Most kids sales were in the $100 to $250 range, very few over $500. The copper tree started with a $100 bid. Prior bids on previous projects were $25 raises. The tree changed at $100 clip. Some people started to clap as the offer passed $1,000, louder as it passed $2,000. People stood and applauded as the bid passed $3,000. Everyone who could stand, stood and cheered as the little copper tree of hope sold for $3,700. At this point, all the wrinkles in this old heart were gone.

How To Treat People

My granddad told me a story many years ago about a farmer plowing with a horse when a man in a buggy stopped beside the field, walked out to the busy farmer and said, "I'm interested in buying land near here. What kind of neighbors will I have?"

The farmer answered, "I guess they are normal. What were they like where you came from?"

"They were great," he said.

"They are like that here too," the farmer said.

The visitor talked a while and then left.

Later that afternoon, a second man in a buggy stopped and the whole process was repeated.

The visitor asked what the neighbors were like. The farmer asked what they were like where he came from.

This time the visitor said, "The whole bunch were awful S.O.B.s"

"They are the same here too," the farmer said, and the visitor left.

"Gramps," I said. "The farmer gave two different answers for the same people."

"Charles, (Gramps always called me Charles) the lesson here is, people treat you like you treat them. Be honest and fair. Life will be good.

He was right.

Traffic Light

Going south on Division, Grand Rapids, Michigan. Talking with passenger. "Nuts, we just ran a red light. Nuts twice, we did it in front of a cop."

The next light was red. We stopped. The police car pulled to the curb. Cop got out of his car. No lights on. Walked into the street up by our driver's window. "Lady you just ran a red light."

"Yes officer, I know."

"Don't you have a light in your town?"

"Truthfully, officer, no we don't."

"Where are you from?"

"Grant."

The light turned green.

"Do you want me to pull to the curb?"

"No, you can go. Don't run any more lights."

We drove away leaving him standing in the center of the street. I guess if you're not used to stop lights, according to him, you're off the hook.

Volkswagon Beetle

Because my driving days are almost over, I'm only giving you folks the short version of this deal. I own a 2001 stick-shift, yellow V.W. Beetle, which my wife drives. She owns a 2000 automatic yellow V.W. Beetle, which I drive. The opportunity arose for her to sell her car, which I drive, so she sold it.

If you don't quite understand all this, I'll put it another way. If you happen to see an old man with a cane, dressed kind of funny, walking down the road, carrying a golf bag, pick me up, will ya?

Thanks!

Pillow Talk

"Neat bedroom."

"It's okay, but it's cold some nights. The days are warm though because we're covered with a bedspread."

"That's good to hear."

"As you see, I'm new here. I wonder why only one pillow was purchased."

"Because the "He" pillows don't last long."

"Really."

"Oh, excuse me, my name is Dud. I'm a pillow factory reject."

"Why my short life expectancy?"

"Long story: First, he has oily skin and stains you."

"Second, His whiskers will wear spots in you."

"Third, he's a boxer. Some nights you will be beaten to a pulp."

"Your only real hope of a life here, longer than three months, is his teeth."

"What? Why?"

"He is a mama's boy. Your only salvation is that his teeth are still in the glass on the sink, when he starts chewing your corners off. Otherwise you're next in line for the dog's bed."

"Does the frequent pillow turnover bother you?"

"No, I'm like a pillow lawyer. I take new pillow cases all the time."

There is a lawyer for everything.

Life Happens, Smile

A very hip, modern dressed young man was sitting in his spotless sports car waiting for the very long and slow moving train to clear the tracks. As he waited, he proceeded to empty all of his ashtrays onto the ground beside his car. Still waiting, he lit a cigarette and relaxed – more ashes on the ground.

His side car mirror revealed that a lady was getting out of the car behind him. The middle-aged woman walked up to his car with a whisk-broom and a small car dustpan. As she cleaned up his mess, she looked at him once with no expression. His look was a smirk as he was thinking, "This is real road service." She was almost done, so he took his last drag on his cigarette and tossed the butt out beside her.

She cleaned it up, stood up, and stepped very close to his car. She smiled; he smirked again. There upon, she dumped the entire contents of her dustpan through his open sunroof window into his immaculately clean car and walked away.

Not a House, a Home

No indoor bathroom, just a pot under the bed. The outhouse was behind the lilac bush (which didn't help much, if you know what I mean.) To get to the cellar we had to go outdoors, open the two cellar way doors, down the steps, open the cellar door to a dirt floor room decorated with cobwebs. Mice had their own private rooms. We had three roof covered cement porches on the east, west and south side of the house. 100 lbs. gas cylinder ran the cook stove. We had to refill the tanks ourselves. No one delivered.

Our heat was from a fuel oil space heater in the living room (with a pan of water on top) the only warm room in the house. No TV, just a big tall radio in the corner which one set on the floor to hear.

My sister died at age six. Inevitably, I was watched like a hawk, protected from everything and loved by the ton. I know it's called being spoiled. But I always felt rich. I knew about the farmer reference to wealth and the pot, and we did have one under the bed.

What?

Each day it came closer, louder, faster, scarier, more dangerous. Heat or cold wouldn't phase it. But if you could stand over it, each time it would always run away. On occasions the sun made it beautiful. It's overpowering force was awesome. The trapped food it left was always appreciated and fun to collect.

1st hint: Did I wet your curiosity?

2nd hint: Here is something fishy about it's description.

Answer: My cup runneth over, but so did Black Creek every spring, next to our house.

Semi Experience

Semi driving was seasonal-flowers and potted trees in spring. I delivered trees to the home of the owner of the Indiana Pacers: flowers to old town Chicago, Illinois. I missed my street on a five-way intersection and couldn't get my semi trailer under the bridge, so I backed the truck through the five way light.

Same city, same trip, had to unload in the middle of the street. The receiver of my goods strongly suggested I lock the cab or I would be robbed while I unloaded.

Hauled bulk cucumbers in summer from Heinz to Bangor, Michigan. As automation unloaded my load my air brakes failed. My truck started down hill. I got from the trailer to cab and stopped it just before it would hit my boss's truck. Just once, I hauled big 4 foot x 8 foot blocks of ice to Chicago to be sculptured for a movie.

In the fall I carried apples and once, I hauled small green tomatoes to Heinz for relish. As I sat waiting for a red light a car pulled beside me. Four men inside, one yelled, "We have a bet on what are you hauling?"

No winners, they all were wrong.

In winter I hauled Xmas trees to Orlando. At the first stop light off the freeway, a beggar walked between vehicles asking for money. The tree buyers told me the beggar owned and lived in a half a million dollar house in the better part of town!

Between Xmas and spring I would take a load of whatever to Florida, deliver it, play golf for a week and bring a load of mulch back to Grand Rapids. On average I would clear at least $200 for the week. Great paid vacation, no expenses period!

Semi Truck to Wisconsin

Mid 1990's, retired from dairy farming. I drove semi part time. My lady friend then, wife now, lived in Wyman. Her closest neighbor, a retired couple also, found out I made trips to Wisconsin. Could the wife ride with me?

The request was granted by my boss. The reasons to ride were many:

1. Husband didn't want to drive that far.
2. Daughter lived there and asked mom to come and see *The Bridges of Madison County* (book and movie.)

3. Last, but not least, mom wanted to ride in a semi.

The daughter gave me the destination point. I gave her the time, 8:00 p.m.

I was 5 minutes late, good trip, great passenger.

What I found out Sunday afternoon at my grandson's going away to college party, the husband shared with me. When he walked into church alone (the couple were always together) "Where is your wife?"

He said, "I told them all at once: She left me two days ago for Wisconsin with a trucker."

Once Upon a C.B.

"I'm a-getten a funny feeling about all this."

"Me too," the C.B. answered.

Wisconsin to Grand Rapids, Michigan was at least a five hour ride in a semi. The fall colors were at their peak. The two C.B.ers seemed nervous about what they observed.

"Ya all look. These trees are dying."

"Ever see anything like this?"

"Heck no, property values must be zero."

"Can't believe people stay here."

"What's killing the trees must affect people's brains."

"I bet that nuclear electric plant on Lake Michigan is making acid rain and doing the killing."

"I betcha some big lumber company is buying the trees already."

"I just rolled up all my truck windows and turned on the inside cabin air."

"I did that 15 miles ago."

"You suppose the company will pay for a blood test?"

"No."

"This is my first and last run to Michigan."

"Me too."

I drove semi part time for five summers. I wish I could remember all they said. Do you think our highways are safe?

Notes

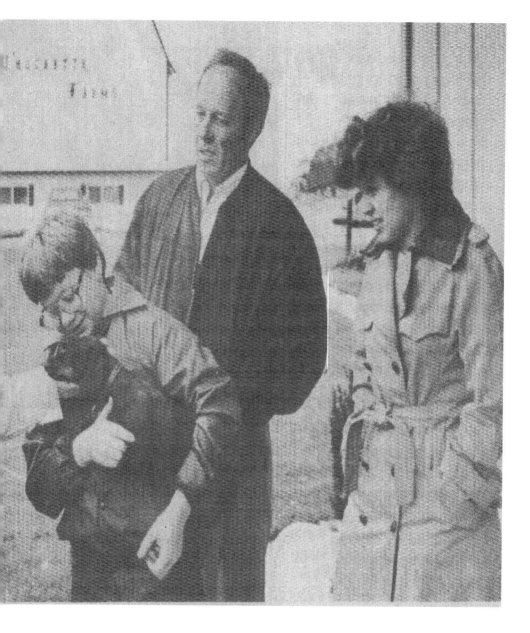

Farming

Farming Changes

Farming has changed much in the 28 years since I retired. The magnitude and specialization of product is unimaginable. But I truly think the quality of character of a farmer has not changed much. If he sees a need, he will cover it.

My old farm of one barn, three silos, toolshed and home is now 10 barns, 3 trench silos and a 40 cow rotary milking parlor. It's a farm town owned and run beautifully by a family from another country. It just couldn't be more, the American experience, than that. I love it.

I have a farmer friend who owns and operated 16,000 acres in 4 states. I'm sure he soon will be adding an airplane to his farm equipment. Come join me as I reminisce about a time when we had to drive the tractor ourselves instead of using G.P.S.

Him, Me and a Fence Post

Moore's on north and south, Ervin's and Walkington's on the east and south, Murray's and Garner's to the west; I was happy with all my farming neighbors. When we stopped our tractors and headed towards our fence line, it usually wasn't because of important information to share. It was our morning "office" break.

Good fences made for good neighbors, but the fence post was the communication link we both would lean on. "The original coffee machine" but with no buttons or choices to make. Our office break gossip covered weather, kids, cows, school sports, who sold out or fell asleep in church Sunday. It wasn't what was said. What is important is we took the time to say it.

P. S. Example of a good neighbor: After breakfast we noticed the neighbor's cows were in our yard. I called and told him. He asked me, "Are you busy?"

"I'm never busy!!"

"Good, please drive them home, will ya?"

I knew he was just kidding, but his new wife didn't. What I heard being yelled by her at him was not repeatable, nor printable. But it was certainly memorable. If I was ever to stoop to bribery I knew who to call.

Once in a while when I share something in private with someone, I say first, "Just between you and me and a fence post."

Chuckette – Chuck It Farms

Thirty-seven year of dairy farming provided many super memories. Granted, I did put up with a lot of "crap." Somehow, being an American farmer meant something to me. I liked it. Efficiency was a necessity to survive. Doing two things at once was super. Not knowing, we picked a farm name with a double meaning: "Chuckette Farms," was my nickname and the second half of my wife's first name.

We soon learned that "Chuckette Farms" covered the good times. But if it was pronounced very fast it also covered the bad times. "Chuck it Farms!"

Cow Pasture

18 acres on the back of the 80 acres was very hilly, with many ponds, making it good for a cow pasture, not crops. One cow was ready to have a calf. I thought I had better check on her.

Farmers never walk if they can ride. I drove the tractor back and into the pasture. As I crested the pasture hill, there she was in the middle of a pond, having her calf. Stupid cow. I hurriedly shut off the tractor, jumped off, and started down the hill. Halfway down, the silent moving tractor passed me about three feet away and slammed into a tree, big enough to stop it cold. I was able to take about three more steps. I had to sit down. My legs wouldn't hold me up. I realized what had almost happened. I said out loud, "Thank you!"

Then I cried.

A Test for Larry K.

1976 was a birthday of sorts for Chuckette Farms. We converted from a conventional stanchion barn to a 100 plus cow loose housing barn with milking parlor. This was before we spoiled cows with merry-go-round moving milking parlors. DeWitt Lumber Company of Blanchard was our builders. We knew every person that DeWitt sent to work on our barn. It made for extra confidence in the builder.

One of DeWitt's summer help was a classmate of my girls. The building was finishing up with the completion of the roof. My wife was gone. The girls wanted to cook dinner for all the builders, kind of a field test of their cooking. Don't bring your lunch tomorrow, guys. Dinner is on us. Roast beef, baked beans, mashed potatoes and gravy, salad, rolls, hot apple pie, choice of drink. It was really good.

After dinner I noticed the high schooler was on his knees, nailing the roof. "Are you all right, Larry?"

"Yes," he answered. "I ate so much I can't bend over. I have to work on my knees."

Dog Bite

Short, dark hair, strong looking, soft-spoken, head and hands were big. If a fight was necessary, I would want to be on his side-kind-of-guy. My milk inspector. He seemed a little different that afternoon. Having been to our farm about a month ago with a companion, why back so soon?

"Did we ship bad milk?"

"No, never," he answered. Silence.

Then he spoke, "Today is my last day of work. I am retiring. I wanted you to be my last and best stop.

And to thank you, because your farm was always my best stop."

I was flabbergasted! I finally got out a "Thank you."

I realized it was not a regular milk inspection. It was a man saying goodbye to his life's work. We relocated to our farm office to sit and talk. I handed him a coke from the barn refrigerator. He reminisced.

I liked this story best. He had just left a farm, which had barely survived the milk inspection. His car drove terrible. He stopped. Two flat tires. The other two also ruined by dog bites. The state had to buy four new tires.

A dog is man's best friend. But a dairy farmer's best friend is a milk-inspector-tire-chewing dog. The story was very popular at all Michigan Milk Annual meetings. It was his favorite story also.

Milking Cows

Dad milked by hand for years. On occasion, the cow would step or kick him. When that happened, his normal rebuttal was punching the animal in the ribs, hurting him much more than the cow. Cows soon learn what not to do.

Mom usually slept on her back; Dad on his side. Dad was dreaming about milking the cow. It kicked. Dad reacted, hitting the animal squarely on the rib. The rib was the pit of mom's stomach, removing most of her air. She couldn't figure out why the sudden loss of air. Dad didn't volunteer a word, but the next day he purchased our first milking machine.

P.S. It was years before mom found out the reason for her unexpected loss of air.

Ouch!

No Mich Con free gas. When we first moved to the farm on Adam's Road we burned coal. The main floor was warm. But my upstairs bedroom wasn't. The more bedcovers, the better. Plus with sweatshirt, pants and socks, you might survive. Sometimes even my nose got cold. Under these extreme conditions the following happened:

I dreamed someone entered my bedroom and was trying to strangle me. I couldn't seem to defend myself as the cold hand moved slowly across my face. I had only one choice- I bit it! Hard! The pain was so intense I screamed.

Woke my folks. The very cold hand was real, leaving many teeth marks, encompassing my right thumb. The very thought of losing body parts prompted me to wear gloves to bed.

Dad commented on our way to the barn, "Son, I think I would suck my thumb instead of biting it. Your call!"

Hot Cars

My 37 years of dairying was spent in the Michigan Consolidated Gas Field around Six Lakes. Almost every landowner had the use of free gas for most all buildings. In the winter, we farmers would migrate from farm to farm and play Euchre. Bring your favorite drink, host furnished food. Farm folks and jokes are synonymous. Our host commented he got into the "Hot Car" business two days prior. "Wow! What did you buy?"

"I didn't buy nothing. The garage furnace stuck on "On." The heat made it to 122 degrees.

Death of a Saleswoman
Business as Usual

Late September afternoon, I was about ¼ done with my evening milking, when the door between the milk house and milking parlor opened. In walked a very attractive lady, dressed like a pill salesperson in a doctor's office. Fur coat and all.

"Mr. Houghton?"

"Yes."

"I represent XYZ Company. Oh Mr. Houghton, this is one of the cleanest milking facilities I've ever been in."

"Thank you. Please tell my milk inspector, will ya? I've never had a visitor wearing a fur coat."

"Well, I believe farmers are the backbone of America. They deserve the best."

A salesperson running for office. She is good. But I think my response floored her. "I'm sorry, lady, I only talk to salespeople from 9:00 to 11:00 on Monday mornings."

She soon realized I meant it.

""Okay, how's 10:15?"

"Great."

She left. Poor soul, she didn't have a chance. The boss would be here at 10:15 and I guarantee she couldn't sell nothing to my wife.

True story. 1978

Thanks Neighbor

Once in a while we get lucky because of circumstances. The first farmer that took over my farm was different. I'm told he beat up a milk inspector and made Mich Con stop working on their pipeline, which ran across the farm, because of too much noise. I built the house he lived in. The noise never bothered us, but Mich Con, for P.R. sake, bought him off.

The damage adjuster from Mich Con called me and gave me all kinds of hell for selling the farm. He said, "The noise never bothered you, but the company said, 'Pay him' so you live twice as close to the work now as he does, so I'm sending you one-third of his payment for noise. Enjoy."

Craig was living with me at the time. We took our "noise money" went to Maxfield's for dinner and stayed all night at the Maxfield's Inn in Edmore.

"Thanks, neighbor!"

Different is Good

My first wife didn't like being married to a farmer. My second wife would not marry a farmer. "No way would I marry a farmer." But of the three, only I loved farming. We agreed in part, but differently on the whole. We all need farmers.

I play golf left-handed. Not many play left-handed I heard, "You're on the wrong side of the ball." and "You make a slice look good." So I might be considered different.

Once, a few years ago at the Birchwood Golf Course, a new league opponent teed it up and hit it farther than I did. He was truly different. He had only one arm. But he played the game with the same result.

When a new type of food is created it's done by mixing in many different ingredients and altered until perfect.

It's a combination of different things that makes up everything. I think different is good, especially with people. What are you made of?

Talkative

I'm a talkative, 78 year old retired dairy farmer. We live quietly south of Remus, Michigan. I count as many of my blessings as I can remember, every day. One of which was attending my first meeting with the "Tamarack Writers Group." It was like being handed the Olympic torch, which I have been trying to "run" with ever since.

Please excuse me for a minute, I have to sit down!

Manure Spreader

My oldest son had different jobs after high school. Once while he was employed at a very large dairy farm, this happened. The farm's manure spreader was one of those very large, open-topped, tub on wheels. On one of the trips to the field, both of the left wheels broke, discharging most of the contents onto the black top, covering an area about 50 feet by 60 feet, and a foot deep with you know what!

The road commission was called and the farmer hurried to get a loader and another spreader to clean up the mess. As he returned with the necessary equipment, the road commission was already there with the "Slow" safety signs. Just as the clean up process started, a young man in a brand new car, totally ignoring the road signs, plowed through the 60 feet of manure at about 40 m.p.h.

The lessons and comments were numerous; all watching had a great laugh:

1. The young man learned, the hard way, to read and heed road signs.
2. He helped the farmer haul away some of the mess!
3. It might have been cheaper to buy interest in the car wash.
4. One of the onlookers commented, "He should take the car back immediately. The deal is beginning to smell!"

Again, much laughter.

Combine Deal

In the first three years after I stopped dairy farming the first buyer turned out to be a little different. One of my fellow farmers filled me in on him. If you did business with him, it was "Cash Only" or you were out.

The story goes this person purchased a very expensive combine but never made a payment on it. He was able to keep the combine hidden from the manufacturer, who had financed the machine. So the manufacturer had the dealer, who sold him the product, inform him there was a recall on it. The farmer thought the dealer was ignorant of the "No Pay" deal, and brought the combine in for recall.

They kept it.

Things To Think About

Lessons From the Deck

As my wife tells me often, "Chuck, if you didn't learn something today, you just weren't paying attention."

She is so right. I would like to share with you what I have learned about life from Mother Nature while sitting on our second story deck. I'm out there every chance I get.

One morning as I was about to enter the deck, I stopped because I noticed 17 buzzards standing in (more or less) formation on the side hill with their wings outstretched. They were drying themselves in the sunlight. It was an awesome sight. Those ugly birds together made for an unforgettably beautiful picture. **Lesson: Look to find the beauty in all things.**

Each spring a big old snapping turtle makes her way slowly across our home-made driving range to lay her eggs. **Reminding me: life can be a long slow uphill road. But it's worth it.**

We see deer everyday on our range. One afternoon in the fall a doe was standing on her hind legs, under the apple tree trying to reach an apple. She stretched out until she was straight up. "Oops!" over backwards she went. "Funny? Yes!" She got up, looked around. The other deer were all watching. I don't know how deer laugh. But I would bet they all did. She didn't quit. She tried again. **Lesson: Set your goals. If you don't succeed, try, try again.**

Deer fawns play tag on our golf greens all the time. **Fun is necessary for a good life.**

Eating breakfast I had a noisy visitor. The hummingbird was about two feet away, looking me right in the eye and complaining. Then I noticed the feeder was empty. My fault. **Lesson: Be responsible and reliable. You will have many friends and too much work.**

I was sitting in the shade below the deck. Our outdoor cat was supposedly sleeping about four feet to my left, when out of nowhere a chipmunk came running at full tilt, jumped over the cat and continued across the golf green. He didn't make it. **Lesson: Tragedy is only a short second away. Be careful of what you do and how you do it.**

Every year a robin builds her nest in the corner of the deck. We often sit and watch her build her home. We also marvel at her worm finding ability. **Lesson: Family First. "A" plus to you all on this one.**

A pair of geese just landed on our pond for the summer. **Just for our military people: It's good to be home!"**

Seems like each year the ground moles pick out one golf green and keep making tunnels under it all the time. We stopped using chemicals and mole traps don't work well. But guess what? A fox took over and solved my problem. He dug them up and disposed of them all. I only had to fill the holes he made. **A helping hand is always appreciated, even when it was actually a paw.**

Each year we leave as many milkweeds as possible for the Monarch butterfly larvae to feed off of. I love to see the Monarchs in flight. **But seeing a person reach their full potential is more rewarding.**

After a rainy afternoon I assumed my favorite spot on the deck. The sun came out bright and created the inevitable rainbow. Wow! The end of the rainbow is in our sand trap by our house. Yes, Mother Nature, I got the message. **Life at the end of the rainbow is as good as it can get.**

Folks, you can't get life lessons from Mother Nature off an app. So seek and you shall find. Take a walk!! Good luck and pay attention.

My Choice

10:36. Good morning world. Got up, picked up my eye drops, morning pills and headed for our deck, hoping not to see our last blade of green grass wilt in the hot sun. My Wonder Woman served cornbread and sausage gravy plus coffee and fruit for breakfast. Restaurants don't know what to serve people.

I ate, then the first of the 3-times-a-day eye drops. Must leave eyes shut for at least 5 minutes. So I listened to my world: cars and trucks on M 66, one quarter mile away. Emma's 4-H pig grunting in her pen. Two birds arguing over tenant's rights. Mother robin talking to her brood from the end of the deck. Our weather vane golfer's high pitch screech as he noted wind direction. I felt the wind. Nice. Look at all the things the wind can do, but it's invisible. Sometimes you must believe in things you can't see. (I've heard that before.) Something warm and smooth against my leg. "Beggar" our cat. Eyes still shut, which one of my senses would I (if I had a choice) give up first and which last?

Boy, I sat and pondered that question a long time. I love to watch people. What they do. The look in their eyes. We judge by looking and sharing thoughts, ideas, creations, triumphs, an "I love you!"

All needed in life. I couldn't choose what to give up first. But this would be the last straw. If for some very unusual reason I could be unable to feel the warmth and love of family and friends, I would have nothing left.

Five minutes are up. What would be your choice?

Mysteries of Life

1. Who put the M.G. car in the Lakeview School hall, only to find it gone when they got to school?
2. How did someone leave a family of little pigs in the Grant School atrium?

3. What band interrupted a semester test at Lakeview School? Clever enough to wire their music into the school's intercom, and even the superintendent couldn't turn them off, nor find them?

4. When was it possible to place a 4' x 8' piece of plywood with the words "Grant Prison" on the front of the Grant School without being caught?

5. Why would some one toilet paper a cop's residence while he sat in his living room in his shorts drinking a beer?

6. What is it like to kiss a preacher's daughter?

7. How it would be to have a nun for your bridesmaid?

8. Which is better? The time you take or the time you give?

9. It's always nice when you have a choice. So what have you got planned for when you don't?

10. We all worry one time or another. I don't think I want to know what it would take for us all to stop worrying at once.

11. I wonder if all clergy of all religions wore the same type of clothes and rotated between churches, mosques or synagogues giving their message. Same use of language: would the parishioners realize the difference?

12. How come thirty years after the fact I learned the top speed of the old pick-up?
13. Who house cleans so thoroughly Q tips are needed for windows?
14. Is a secret really a secret just because no one talks about it?
15. Why didn't someone tell me grandmothers got better-looking as I got older?
16. Who would go to a fancy restaurant and only eat deviled eggs?
17. If you don't die you get older. What's the perk side of that?
18. What makes you wiser? Asking a question to confirm your opinion, or to learn something new?

Two Times

"Bang!"

The gun discharged, bullet entering his stomach area. Practicing spinning a pistol and slipping it into your holster works much better if you unload the gun first. Being very manly he didn't call the ambulance. Instead, slowly he entered his pickup and drove the 10 miles to the nearest hospital.

Realizing he was probably 0-2 on making wise decisions, the E.R. people were all over him for driving wounded. But after many tests and X-rays it was determined the bullet never hit any vital organ.

The discharging doctor commented, "You are certainly a lucky man. I hope you learned something from all this."

His answer, "Yes, I have. Over the last two years I've become a much better shot. Because when I tried the trick the first time, I shot myself in the foot."

Walmart

Mrs. J.M.H. would you please pick up your children at our information desk. The name was correct, but this is strange. She hurried to the desk. On arrival she discovered her 30 and 34-year- old sons had used the unattended desk to locate mom instead of looking all over Walmart for her.

Diplomacy

I have encountered some very wise and thoughtful people in my lifetime, but this response to a delicate question gets the gold medal for diplomat of the year. I totally love this man. Both divorced. Together now for some time, this tidbit came rolling out of him one sunny afternoon. He said,

"She said, "I can't imagine what you find attractive about me. My bust line is almost zero!"

"Wait a minute," he answered. "Your bust line is really a plus."

He led her out to his woodshed. "You're a beautiful woman. Hon, please extend your arms. Thank you."

As he loaded her arms with sticks of wood, he smiled and said, "Because of your build, you're at least two small pieces of wood or one bigger piece better than any woman I know!"

Gold medal please!

Character

Together, your parents raised you to survive on your own by teaching good judgment. Does something look right? Sound right? But personality, does it feel right?

Living with choices made is a big slice of life. Everything you say or do is a judgment call, almost all the time, whether by you or by other people about you. Everyone can handle the good times. How you handle the rough times determines character and quality of life. You leave an impression on all people, all the time. It's a big part of life.

I believe we learn from our mistakes. The harder you try, the more mistakes you'll make. But look at how much more you'll learn.

"Attitude" opens doors. Ability keeps them open. Hint: always do your best. You never know who's watching. The very few times you'll need to stand up alone and be counted, will be your proudest.

The secret of life is the process of living it. Enjoy yourself. Knees are a vital support when asking for guidance. Bend them often. Very soon I know, I'll be leaning back in my favorite chair with a big, big smile reading the TV's top five book releases with one authored by Katherine Moore!

(I wrote this for college-bound Katherine but thought it is good for all potential students.)

Phil D. – On Unions

When I was elected to the Montabella School Board, unions were just starting up in the school. The first to strike were the bus drivers. Our board and drivers were having many meetings. During a break in negotiations, Phil D., the high school principal, and I were discussing the matter.

He commented on the wisdom of the union. "They are doing it all wrong."

"Why?" I asked.

The reply: "Drivers strike, teachers will drive bus or parents bring the kids to school. Cooks strike; kids carry their lunch. Custodians strike, teachers clean their room and buy toilet paper. If the union was on top of this, they would have the secretaries strike. The whole school system would shut down in two days!"

Education

Education is so very important. It makes a profound difference in one's life. Look at me, the result of multiple college degrees. Oh, I didn't go to college. I went to the barn, so all my four kids could go. Now they take care of me. My specialty was in adult care, because of the retirement program

Just Think

Don't judge another man until you have walked in his shoes. Chances are his shoes won't fit; they'll hurt. So your judgment will be off, right from the start.

Being realistic or being negative is really a double-barreled shotgun. Where your shot hits your target determines whether it hurts or not. Choosing your words carefully keeps you in office, but probably won't endear you to anyone. I know, I was right once, when I told my wife I was wrong.

The only true way to win an argument is don't have one. *Telling the truth* doesn't always create happiness. But wouldn't it be great if it always did? Have you noticed if you look at the world with a smile, it looks better?

If you can't hold your anger any longer, go off by yourself and let go, being assured there will be no repercussion if you're wrong. It works. The big difference between being happy and mad: mad puts a big limit on who you can talk to, or who wants to talk to you!

Play Ball!

The Moores and Me

Theron, Duane and Irv Moore were my baseball-playing neighbors in the 1950s. They had built a backstop in their cow pasture. We had a place to play.

Rules were simple: with only two on a team

1. Right-handed batters had to hit the ball left of second base; reverse that for left-handed hitters. Hit a ball to wrong field, you were out.
2. Pitcher called balls and strikes.
3. If you didn't get your teammate home to score he came to bat and you went to his base.
4. No base stealing.
5. If your hit ball got to the pitcher before you got to first, you're out.

Theron and Duane always played Irv and I. This was the greatest baseball practice I could ever get. I personally felt if I could occasionally hit Theron's fastball or Duane's curve ball, which were a cow-stained green, thrown at twilight, I would never have a problem with a regular baseball.

Fair Play

Playing baseball was always fun for me. The spirit of fair play happened during a time out. I was pitching for Lakeview in our league championship, an extra important game. I delivered a strike to the left-handed batter. Ump called, "Strike three, batter's out."

The batter protested, "It's only two strikes!"

The batter's coach called, "Time!" and the disagreement continued.

My catcher came to the mound. "Ump called him out on two strikes! Hot dog!"

I asked, "Would you like to be out on two strikes?"

The ump stopped talking. Yelled, "Next batter. Play ball."

I called time out and asked for the ump. He met me halfway. I said to him, "You are one of the best umps I have ever pitched for. But the batter only has two strikes."

He took off his mask, looked at me, turned towards the other team's dugout, and yelled, "Get that left-handed batter with two strikes back to the plate."

I was surprised I was the only person who could change the ump's mind. Much praise was given me by their coach, my coach, the crowd and the batter. We won the game, but we won fair and square. That was the best part.

It's the way you play the game that counts the most! I remember why and how it happened, but not the score.

Uncle Cecil's Team

My Uncle Cecil had a baseball team that played at Valley Field in Grand Rapids. My dad was a member of the team, even though, because of work, he couldn't always play. The story goes Dad didn't get to the game until it was almost over.

Score tied. Uncle's team had a runner on third. He called timeout. Short talk. Pat on the back. Uncle sent dad in to run. First time the two teams had played. They weren't familiar with each other. So when the runner at third was replaced by a very short, 5'3", short-waisted, short-legged, bald-headed, old-looking person, the pitcher and catcher pretty much forgot about him.

Uncle had noticed that the catcher always lobbed the ball back to the pitcher standing behind the mound. (Remember the short talk?) Dad took note of the catcher's routine. So on his second ball return, dad took off for home. Scored standing up. The losing team just learned Dad had never lost a foot race.

Be careful when you judge people.

A Scrimmage to Remember

When I was in the seventh grade at Six Lakes School, it was decided to hold a scrimmage baseball game for the seventh and eighth graders between Six Lakes and Lakeview schools. We didn't have a field for baseball so we went to Lakeview. As I previously

106

stated, it was a scrimmage game, so everyone got to bat.

I was a long way from being a starter on our team. However, near the end of the game I got my first ever chance to bat. Our coach was the fifth grade teacher, Mr. Ben McComb. He called me up to bat. We stood in front of the dugout with his hand on my shoulder.

He said, "Chuck, the pitcher is a little wild, so just stand there, don't swing, and you'll probably walk."

We didn't have starter sports way back then. Boy was I excited. I stepped to the plate remembering everything the coach said. I swung at the first three pitches, missed them all, and walked slowly back to the dugout.

Coach McComb, forever the positive teacher, walked down to where I was sitting and said, "Chuck, I know this is your very first game. I was amazed by your grasp of where the strike zone is exactly. Every pitch you swung at I thought was a ball."

Teachers are great, aren't they?

You Never Know Who's Watching

My oldest son, Chris, and I were talking the other day. Out of the blue he said, "Dad, I've never forgotten the example you gave me for always doing the best you can all the time because you never know who is watching."

In 1955, I was a 10th grader. I had been trying out for the varsity baseball team. After two weeks of practice, coach Cook gave out the suits. I did not get one. I was disappointed. It was my last day of baseball for 1955. Coach Cook asked me to pitch batting practice. Now, pitching batting practice and throwing batting practice are two totally different things to me.

The first five batters were all baseball suit recipients. They had a lot of swings, but no hits. I hadn't paid attention as to who was watching practice until the 6th batter came to bat. It was Coach Cook. He said, "Pitch to me."

I threw the same kind of pitch three times. He hit a pop up to the catcher. Coach Cook smiled and said, "Chuck, I didn't give out all the suits today. There are two left and you just earned one of them!"

My son remembered it all quite well. I personally follow the policy yet today. The difference being that once you get married, you know exactly who is watching.

P.S. I always wondered if Coach Cook planned that day, or if it just happened that way!

A Note from Chuck
Blanchard, Michigan

July 30, 1957

Dear Ann,

Well guess who. Yup, it's me. I finally got around to write. I never receive any mail from Grand Rapids. You'd think the place had disappeared.

I got my annual the other day. It's pretty good, if I say so myself. (snob)

I went up and tried out for the Tigers. It was a lot of fun. I met Pat Mullon and talked with him for a long time. I pitched two innings, struck out four men and allowed no hits and in one time at bat I got a home run and after it was all over, I had my picture taken with Pat Mullon.

Harold Gorby and I, with some boys from Mt. Pleasant, went to Flint, July 20th and played in the Hearst Tournament. Sixteen boys were picked out of all the boys there and both Harold and I were lucky enough to go on and play again. Well enough of the hot air.

Tiger Stadium

Going on, the next stop was playing in Tiger Stadium. I had just turned 18. Still didn't have to shave. Baseball was king in the 1950s. I don't know if I won or lost the draw, but I was first to pitch for our group.

My emotions were off the chart. "So if I'm dreaming, please don't wake me up," covered for the day. As I readied myself to pitch, I found my folks seated second row, third baseline. Dad was smiling ear to ear. I nodded. They waved.

"Play ball!" the ump ordered. My first pitch, a ball. My second pitch bounced twice before it hit the center field wall for a triple. "Welcome to Tiger Stadium, Chuck."

I looked at my dad; he was still smiling! From our years of baseball together, I knew what he was thinking. "These guys are really good son. You can't throw it by them. So outsmart them."

My lifetime favorite baseball memory!

Thanks, Dad, thanks for everything.

Take One for the Team!

After I graduated from high school, I was asked to play for the Lakeview Independent baseball team. They had extra good ball players like Helms, Stine, Draine, and so on, which meant I could learn much about the game.

My first game as a member was against Morley at Morley. I rode over in my friend Bill Hall's convertible. Got both sun and wind burned. I guess Morley was short of pitchers that Sunday because after about four innings we were up 15 to 0.

The team managers had a meeting, after which, Harry Helms approached me in the dugout.

"Chuck, get warmed up. You're going to pitch."

Oh good, I was ready, I thought. Harry was still standing, He then pointed at the Morley dugout.

"Oh", he said. "You're pitching for Morley!"

After the roar of laughter subsided, what I had just learned was, besides a sacrifice bunt, I had just become the first sacrificed pitcher!

Notes

Good Home Towns

Sportsmanship

I smile when I say, "I graduated from Lakeview High School." A miracle I made it. Schools reflect the standards of the communities and vice-versa. Lakeview's standards have always been high, sportsmanship being one of them.

Some 62 years ago I was sitting in a Mt. Pleasant gym, waiting. Our game was second. The first game was between an area team and an Upper Peninsula team. The U.P. support was limited to ball team, cheerleaders and a few parents. It was obvious U.P. had two very good basketball players. Referees were far more lenient on verbal abuse and taunting then. It was win at all cost for the home area school.

It was not pretty to watch. The U.P. kids kept their cool against the odds. The Lakeview crowd didn't like the odds either. We started cheering for the U.P. so much so, that by half time, the U.P. cheerleaders were moved to in front of us to cheer.

Did the Lakeview crowd make a difference? Well the U.P. came from behind and won going away. I thought so. Lakeview lost a great semi-final game that year (1956). The U.P. team won it all. "State champs!"

1957 was Lakeview's year!

P.S. *My* class!

Editorial

I know a lot of people from Edmore and I like every one of them. Between Edmore people and surrounding potato farmers we have been able to raise more than $42,000 for the Children's Miracle Network and the M.S. Foundation. I thank you all for that. Even though I now live next to Remus, we still do much business with Edmore Maxfields, Miller's Insurance, Irv's Family Food and of course, my summer home, The Links of Edmore. Your town has more to offer than most because of the Curtis Foundation. Just look at the college support Montabella seniors receive from it.

Success is determined much by the management of assets. I will share the following.

Second year of twelve years on the Montabella School Board we hired a new superintendent. In his first year, a well-respected lady teacher made a request for funds to attend a meeting for educational purpose. The new super gave his reasons why it wasn't necessary!

The School Board voted 7 – 0 in favor of the teacher. The super was visibly upset, and asked for an immediate closed session of the board. He got it. His statement, "You voted 7 – 0 in her favor. Am I on my way out already?"

We answered, "Heck no! We just didn't agree. You run the school, we will judge how and which way you do it."

He instituted answering the school phones with, "It's a great day at Montabella."

I would like to hear, "It's a great day in Edmore."

Thank you.

Tee Time

Edited by Emma Murray, who also gave me the golf ball with the clock for my birthday.

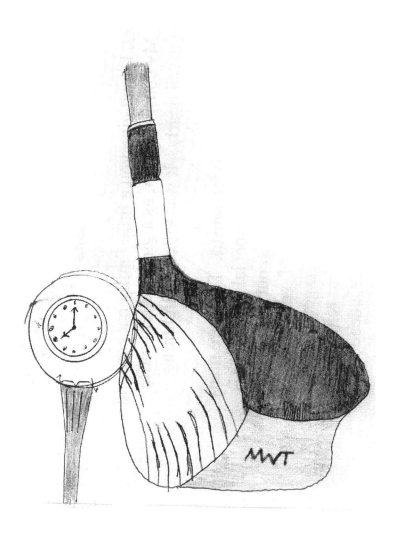

The Perfect Swing

I stepped upon the perfectly groomed grand
And gazed at the immaculate created land
Which I soon would surely band
With this golf ball in my hand.
Helped by the rush of confidence in my soul
I knew how far the ball would roll.
With the perfect swing and the perfect grip
With all my strength I let her rip.
"Oh my! What just happened to me?"
My golf ball is still on the tee.

The only poem I ever submitted for a contest. I won.

Why I Golf

I enjoy all aspects of the game. Teeing it up sets the stage for all the surprises it offers. I never play mind games with my opponent. I cheer for them. I personally know what a great shot does for your spirit.

If a fist bump or a "High Five" is deserved I make sure it's done. Fun is one of my goals. Almost all of my competitors at Pilgrim's Run are busy, active, working, younger people. They refer to me with all the references to old people. Not long ago, after the match was over, one of these people pulled off his golf glove, removed his hat, shook my hand, and said, "You know gramps, I would rather lose to you than beat any team in our league."

Again, why I play golf.

Just the nature of this game played correctly will make a better person out of you. Please enjoy some of the things that impressed me.

A Time Before Golf

In a time before golf, we bowled. It was spring time, a fellow team member passed this tidbit along about life.

He awoke to soft music from the record player. His wife was noticeably busy in the bathroom, which she soon exited, wearing a negligee and not much else. Hair was combed, make-up on, walking slowly to the bed, big smile, sliding her hand gracefully across the foot of the bed up to his side to a face-to-face position. Strong perfume was evident. Slowly she kissed him passionately,. With her hot breath on his ear she whispered, "April Fool!" and took off for the kitchen.

Don't Judge People

Don't judge people until you've played a round of golf with them a few times. Each round will show maybe wisdom, skill, creativity, alcoholism, social skills, his opinion of women, value of money, political views, love of jokes or racism.

Does he try to impress you with his $499.99 driver or his garage sale discovery? Is his foot wedge accurate, or does he hit it where it lies? Can he count strokes, or did he fail math in school? Is golf a game or life and death? Does he explain why he missed the shot, twice? Is he a golf pro who tells you what to do and how to do it with only one golf lesson under his belt? Does he have a reason why for everything that goes wrong?

Are the "gimmies" longer for older people? Does he show patience with slow players, and give much praise and seem to enjoy himself? Is he fun to be with, and would you loan him a $100.00? Or would you have him babysit your kids? Would you like to be marooned on an island with him? This is my screening process. Did you pass?

Some People Play Golf and Do Business

Some people play golf and do business all at the same time. Golf is a character check. Playing alone and solving a personal problem also works well. There is a ton of ways to play for money, which is a very popular thing to do. A family foursome of golf is in a class all by itself. Playing in a golf league with a group of golfers is something to cherish. The truly fun things which occur on occasion while playing the game are my favorite memories.

One comes to mind. Three of us were standing on the Links of Edmore fourth tee, waiting on the fourth person to tee off. He being notorious for time taken to launch the ball. Change his grip. Move his feet. Adjust the height of ball on tee. Close eyes to meditate. Check wind direction by watching cigarette smoke. Adjust shirt. God help us if a fly lit on the ball. He would brush it away and start all over!

But this was our day I'll never forget. He was about halfway through his second round of teeing off when we heard the very loud and annoying buzzing sound. We turned to our great delight, one person had brought his portable electric razor, knowing he had time to shave during the tee off ritual.

Yes it happened! It's my favorite golf story.

The two main people in this true story are lifetime friends. They have a picture of themselves sitting in lounge chairs by a swimming pool with each one having a cold one in hand. The picture very clearly shows a cobweb from one man's shoulder to the other's shoulder. "They were bonding."

Special People

The part of golf that will always resonate with me isn't the ball in flight it's the feet on the ground, watching it disappear. Son Craig and I try to play one fund-raising golf tournament per month, using only family members to round out the foursome. It's as good as it can get for me.

Also, each summer, Kevin and Todd, owners of "Innovative Property Tax Solutions," a multi-state company, take my son and his choice of guest, *"me,"* to a top golf course in the tri-state area, all expenses covered, plus great golf attire. Making the day extra special is a trophy they furnished, which bounces back and forth from the right-handed Todd and Craig to left-handed Kevin and I. Being humble left-handers, we realize the extra pressure the possibility of being beaten by two lefthanders in one day can be, so we have been known to back off a little and lose by a couple of strokes. "Thanks, guys, you're the best!"

Our Golf Course

The house burned in December of '99. Gaylen built the replacement in 2000. When it was completed he asked, "Chuck, would you like a couple of golf greens out there?"

The five-acre field east of the new house was perfect for golf: hills, trees, tall grass, ponds. Our course expanded to six golf greens and one regular grass green. Gaylen's constant course improvement climaxed with a marvelous putt-putt course.

We have had many visitors over the years:

1. Two exchange students
2. Five high school golf coaches
3. Six golf course owners
4. One teacher from the highest academic rated private funded international high school in the U.S. They had students from all over the world located in Georgia.
5. We were honored by the Chippewa High School boys and girls golf teams coming to practice many times. Montabella High School also.
6. We held two tournaments: The Double Mulligan. On 10-19-2015 Larry Halsey aced our 178 yard "Kim's Corner" green.

Our course was designed to accommodate any shot you wanted to practice. Not many even wanted to try our "Shot From Hell." It consisted of a downhill tee off in the trees, over a pond, between two trees, over a hill 141 yards to a blind small green fronted by a grass pond, out of bounds three yards left, a tree-filled gulley four yards behind and down hill slope from the green right. Your only hope was to hit the electric wires in the middle so you got another shot.

Game of Golf

I enjoy the game of golf. If I played the game for blood, a transfusion would be needed at least once a week. I revel at a great shot, no matter who hits it. I love it.

Last night in our golf league my opponent made 3 putts from over 25 feet and one from the fringe of more than 30 feet. I thanked him for making my day. The score was tied. I couldn't pass up my favorite line, "Hey man, there is no glory in telling people you just beat a 78-year-old, half-blind, handicapped golfer.

Or

When I was asked if I would play golf next year, I answered, "I should quit for humanitarian reasons. The humiliation of you young folks being beaten by a 79-year old, half-blind cripple that you have to pick up the ball for, would be hard for me to endure and unbearable for you."

A Good Memory

September 2018 – last night of Pilgrim's Run Men's Golf League: much liquid cheer, laughter and harassing.

I usually converse on these occasions. Tonight was different. We finished our chicken or steak. Our year-end meeting started. New officers were elected. Then the question, "Who's not coming back next year?"

As my hand slowly went up it seemed like part of me disappeared, lost forever. My son sat next to me. "Craig, how many years of golf together?"

"Just an even 30 years, dad."

I was sad inside but I was very thankful because I was able to play league golf all year with each son this time. To me I aced my last year of golf. And my daughter helped make it possible.

That's My Boy

Chance opportunity will reveal how we are doing as a parent. We are honored each year when the local high school golf team comes to practice. Some parents accompany the kids to watch. We talk. I learn much after the session is over. The kids pick up the 300 to 500 balls. "Let's see if my son is learning anything," a dad mentioned, as the ball retrieving began.

If the boys pick up on the way out meant they carried all the weight all the way back. Not smart.

Only three golfers went out and picked up. Coming back. Good job, dad. His kid was one of the three.

P.S. You never know who's watching.

Perfect Golf:
Mulligan Please

I have been through Hell a couple of times, so I thought I would try golf in heaven, and it would go like this, I think:

1. All fairways would be downhill and slope to the center.
2. Domed sand traps and the ball never plugs.
3. Golf ball rejecting ponds; the balls bounce on and then off.
4. Wind is always at your back.
5. No divots to fix. The ground returns to normal in 10 seconds.
6. The ball will beep if it is lost.
7. All your clubs will reject hitting the wrong ball.
8. Cups are twice as big in heaven.
9. You have a choice of one, either "an ace" or a double eagle, one per week.
10. Players keep their scores on a card in the cart, but actual scores, including toe wedge, missed swings, etc. are electronically scored in the clubhouse. The course will give door prizes to

11. "Poor Memory" players whose card score comes closest to the actual clubhouse score.
12. There is a weekly contest for who can toss a golf club the farthest. Also, a free massage for any tosser with a sore arm. (This is a different take on "Anger Management.")
13. Golf cart T.V. will automatically announce an excuse for a screw up. (This will save a lot of whining.)
14. If you play too slow, your ball will propel itself forward 50 yards and a stroke will be added electronically in the clubhouse.

Heavenly Perks

1. If you don't want to play this course, enter the clubhouse and ask for Joe Passov list of Top 100 Courses of the World. Tell lady in charge what number golf course you want. Go to the first tee and you are there.
2. No tee times in heaven. Start any time.
3. You can order anything from the cart person and they will have it.
4. You never have to pay your credit card bill.
5. You can drink all you want with no effect.
6. You can't hit anyone; the ball will automatically stop 10 feet away.
7. All cuss words will register as praise in the clubhouse.

8. All carts have a joke book! Enjoy!

Ladies:
Same as men, plus the following:
1. You can use polka dot tees after 70.
2. You can electronically pick any pro golfer or instructor from Golf magazine for shot advice, instead of husband.
3. If lady is a walker, she can have her choice of any t.v. or movie star for a caddie.
4. If you are losing badly, the match will be called because of rain.

Golfing in heaven will be fantastic; to finish my train of thought, because in heaven, as on earth, they will have Golf Magazine. The difference up there will be that the instructors give the lessons live and for free and they will try not to laugh. The rules guy won't throw the book at you either because it's heaven, and rule # 117.63A states, "No throwing of books allowed in Heaven. Period. Thank you God.

Sorry, I have to stop dreaming about golf in heaven and slow my car down because I'm going through Hell, Michigan, for the third time.

Mixed Emotions

Mixed Emotions

Folks, I must give you a little family background for this. My cousin's mom, as a girl, had a favorite horse she loved dearly. It was killed by lightning. Devastating.

A sweetheart of a sister cousin. There are many reasons why she is on my extra special list. Here is one. Once in a while, she needed to put her brother in place. Oldest brother, college prof, very smart, great guy. But occasionally, he would get carried away on something. She would need to remind him. "Remember, Ned, you got named after a dead horse!"

Aunt Ruby and Mom Hunting

Mom loved to hunt; her next older sister didn't care much about it. But with a considerable amount of coaxing she finally agreed to go. The family had a farm on the south side of Fifth Lake. It was decided they would rabbit hunt from the barn down to the lake swamp grass. Also the stump fences provided much cover for rabbits. After the third rabbit was flushed from its hiding spot, mom noticed her sister never shot. "Why not, sis?"

The reply, "You asked me to go hunting with you. Nothing was said about shooting anything, so I didn't bring any shells."

No she wasn't a blonde.

First Day of Deer Hunting

First day of deer hunting season, early 1980's, my hired help was gone hunting, so I was all alone in the milking parlor. In walked my father-in-law, brother-in-law, uncle and his son. The weather that day was sleeting rain and windy, a totally miserable day. "What are you four up to?"

"We're going deer hunting."

"No way! On a day like this?"

"It's deer season! You go regardless!"

"Okay guys, tell me the truth. Would you go to work on a day like this?"

"You're kidding, Chuck, you'd have to be nuts to work on a day like this!!"

My prognosis: they were in the final stages of "Buck Fever!"

Dear Dad and Deer

I sat in the old Oldsmobile with dad, on his last day ever to hunt deer and watched as he was able to fill four farm deer permits. All you deer hunters understand this, so I'll say no more.

Before I left the farm, I planted the non-farmable back 18 acres to pine trees and I left three deer strips for hunters, in honor of mom and dad.

American Pride

Deer hunting in central Michigan wasn't good until after the 1980's, so my folks always went north for the annual event. Their favorite spot was Eight Point Lake. Mom had first pick on where to sit. This time dad picked a tree planted area. As he walked the rows of pines he discovered a deep hole, man made, with a seat in it. Sitting on the seat, only dad's head was above ground level. The view under the trees was great; he stayed in the hole.

Later the fun began. A doe walked up beside the hole. She could smell dad (he was only a foot below her.) He was enjoying her frustration. A scary thought hit him, "What if someone shoots at the deer?"

"Miss low, and I'm shot, no way. Dad's rifle barrel was just below the doe. He poked her with it. Her get-away leap was straight into the nearest pine. Dad had a different kind of deer story to tell. But very memorable. **He hit the deer, but didn't shoot his gun!**

No Way!! Really?

Unbelievable things do happen! You learn to live with it. Accept it, okay? This family folklore is an heirloom I can repeat with pride.

We listened to tales of shooting prairie dogs ¼ mile away, my Dad shooting a buck 13 times and ending up cutting its throat to seal the deal. As a teenager hunting just north of King's Corners, I awoke from a sound sleep to see a 10 point buck smelling my feet. I shot, no luck. (I never hold my gun when I sleep.)

Almost all hunting stories involve males. Not this time! In the late 1950's mom and dad lived and farmed on Adams Road. One afternoon in duck season, mom took her single barreled, 20 gauge shotgun and walked to the pond at the back of the farm. Using the brush as cover, she got very close to the pond. The ducks spooked and started to fly. She fired her one and only shot. <u>Three</u> ducks fell dead into the water. A fourth duck, hit in the wing, fell on the other side of the pond and tried to run. Mom ran it down. The duck-hunting trip didn't last 25 minutes. As she carried four ducks into the house, what a smile she smiled. No more talk about who was the best shot! Mom cooked the ducks, but Dad and I ate crow!

What makes this story so special is the very old gun mom used had a sawed off barrel with a hole drilled for a matchstick sight. So folks, Dad and I got a heaping helping of crow that day.

Describe an airplane ride to your great-great-great grandparents

Look, Great-great-great-great, if you have ever been unlucky enough to see a tornado up close you will notice many objects floating in the air, going along with the storm. The noise is very intense. So let's pretend you are sitting in a courting chair, with your spouse seated back-to-back in your parlor but the parlor is floating in the storm, high in the air. Let's pretend someone is able to operate the storm, raise you, parlor and all, up and down and travel at 10 times the speed of a horse. Set you, your spouse, back on the ground 300 miles from home in about an hour. As the storm leaves you and yours standing all by yourself in a field.

Note: You just made history by being the first people ever to miss your flight home and you can't call for pick-up because the horses got loose. Phone ain't invented yet.

Pontoon Boat

My wife's family are hunters and fishermen and have many stories to tell. But this is the best. As they headed down the hill to our lake to fish there was their pontoon boat still afloat, but just barely. A beaver had chewed off a very large tree, which landed squarely on the pontoon, mashing some of the railing and the console. I bet you could ask your know-it-all phone, "What are the odds on a beaver bombing a pontoon boat with a tree?" It couldn't answer. I think I'll call Farmers Insurance to see if they would have covered it!

Kids!

22 hours of labor furnished us with our first son; all was good. Hospitals kept mothers at least 24 hours 50 years ago, so I went home. Plus picking up our 5 and 6 year old daughters from Grama's. Excitement was running rampant. Getting them to sleep was impossible. They wanted their new bro home with them. I finally gave up. In bed with dad, "Whoopie!"

Questions, questions, no let up. Being awake more than 24 hours I was at their mercy. Girls, girls, we have to sleep. My 6 year old said, "Okay daddy, we'll try to. It would help if you would whisper in my ear, like you do with mommy sometimes."

Oh heck yes, I mumbled something in her ear, where upon she sat up in bed, crossed her arms and said, "No! No! No! I washed and ironed all day and I'm tired."

It worked. We all went to sleep. (smart kid)

P.S. I quietly laughed myself to sleep.

Six Lakes School

Grade school at Six Lakes began for me as a second grader. My mother was hired as the fourth grade teacher. I rode to school with her. Being a teacher's kid in the same school just isn't a cakewalk in the park. My mother used me for all kinds of disciplines and experiments, not that I ever needed discipline.

Well, maybe a couple of times. As a fifth grader we boys were involved in a snowball fight in front of the school so intense the librarian didn't dare to enter the school. Our fifth grade teacher stepped out the door and caught a snowball just above the left ear. He slowly wiped the snow from his head. Not being a vindictive person, he said, "I don't even want to know who threw that snowball. It doesn't matter. You all have lost all your recesses for the rest of the week."

I thought he was fair. I didn't want to sit out the week all alone.

My First Job

"Charles, I think you should try to earn some money for school clothes."

Mothers always have great ideas. "Gee whiz, mom, I can't drive. I do have a bicycle. Where can I work?"

"Right here at home. We'll plant ½ of the garden to cucumbers – you can pick them and we'll take them to Crawford's Pickle Station to sell."

This was serious work at age 10; I didn't even like play if it was hard to do. As farmers call it, picking pickles is only part of picking pickles. You must
1. Windrow the vines.
2. Pull all the weeds.
3. Never leave the vine upside down.

4. Any previous missed pickles must be picked and discarded.

Your only boss is the almighty dollar. The more you pick, the more you make. $18.00 bought a lot of clothes in 1949. Making a maze on the front lawn with a push mower was much more fun than picking pickles.

Walking to Church

Walking to church has a pleasant ring to it. One-eighth of a mile was a perfect distance. Stretch your legs. Love the moment. Our kids did. The U.B. church on Adams Road has a long history of serving the community. No basement, so Bible School was held across the road in the parsonage. One day after I was appointed to finish the Millbrook Township clerk's term, the road commission started black-topping Adams Road. (Boy, did I get kidded about that.)

Okay, back to church. So because of the new road, traffic was faster. The commission, realizing the kids crossed the road, put a new sign between us and church. "Slow Children" was put in place.

Our first Sunday after the sign was put up, the family was off to church. My youngest son took off running. Our daughter caught him. "See the sign?" she yelled, "Slow children."

"Walk!"

Changed Churches

My daughter and son-in-law changed churches many times, looking for an answer to their needs. Their prayers, they felt, were answered by a religion which had no tolerance for anything which deviated from the Bible's scripture. Especially, we are all created equal. All their church's floral arrangements were purchased at my daughter's place of employment. She noticed some orders for certain church members were far more expensive than other member's orders. She brought the matter to the attention of the church. They totally ignored it. My children quit that church.

Religion can't change faith. But faith can change religion sometimes.

Religion

Religion survives on numbers. Faith exists in units of one. Religion looks for you. By contrast, you find faith. Religions are different; true faith is constantly the same for all. We dress for religion, but are naked in the faith. Religions try to impress with the structures they build; the best sermon I ever heard was in a man's garage. No offering. Religion must be taught; faith never is.

Religion is recognized by assimilation. Faith is yours alone. Religions want you to make a choice on which is best. With true faith there is no need to choose. No religion covers all of man's needs, but true faith does. *I'm sorry, please forgive me. Can I help? Call anytime. Yes, I will. I love you!* These are phrases of faith. I hope you hear them often or use them.

Jim Bear
Church in Garage, Free Thanksgiving Dinner

Jim Bear, 6 foot, handsome, very pleasant, good, dedicated to mankind's welfare, drove school bus for C.M.U., ordained minister. He didn't only preach the gospel, he lived it, rare personality trait. If you shared something with him, you knew it was still your secret, kind of man. Bible study in his garage. No offering taken. His R.N. wife backed him all the way, a united front.

I have a grandson going to a divinity college in the south. I asked him one day, "Chase, why do we seem to lose mostly super-good people way too early, and the characters survive?"

His answer, "God don't want the characters, either, Gramp."

A Thanksgiving Treat

One of the best parts of being a grandparent is giving advice or, if I may say, preaching to a grandchild. We, with many years of accumulated wisdom enjoy dispensing some. It's our "right of passage."

Last Sunday, I had the opportunity to attend church. The sermon was given by my grandson. He was home on break, from a southern divinity college. Sitting there absorbing wisdom and direction "from" him, was unprecedented and a very enjoyable experience. He was good and now he's got a "50 year" head start on me. I think the world is going to make it.

My Thanksgiving came early.

Amen.

Family

Let's Pray

Life After Lori

Note: After means after.

We had just moved from an upstairs apartment to an old house on M-66 when life after Lori began.

Age 37 months, first time:

There was a knock on the door. The wife answered, "Yes?"

"Do you have kids?"

"Yes, they are upstairs playing."

"Not all of them. Please check upstairs now."

My wife rushed upstairs to find Lori had opened the window and was sitting on the windowsill with her feet outside. It was a 16-foot drop.

Second time:

Knock on the door.

"Do you have kids?"

"Yes, why?

"Because there is a little girl riding down the center line of M-66 on a tricycle."

It was Lori. She had gotten from the house into the garage, opened a side door, got her bike, and went for a ride.

Third time:

It was bath time. My wife put Lori in a small amount of water, and went to get her sister as she was after our second child. She heard the vacuum cleaner start up. She rushed back to the bathroom to catch Lori finish sucking all the water out of the tub. (The vacuum was in storage.)

Fourth time:

It was back when people ironed clothes, and my wife finally got it finished. She put the iron away, and went about finishing supper. By now, it became apparent that watching Lori was almost a full-time job all by itself. Even though the house was locked down, you had to check every two minutes or so. My wife smelled smoke – which did happen once in a while. She rushed to the living room to find the plugged in iron on the best chair with the shape of the iron burned all the way to the springs of the chair.

Fifth time:

It was high school graduation time, prom time, etc. My cousin and his girlfriend stopped by on their way to the prom. The girl had on a beautiful prom dress. She thought Lori was so cute, so she picked Lori up and sat her on her lap. Lori was bring potty trained and didn't have diapers on. We know what happened next, don't we? Lori messed all over the girl's lap.

Shortly after, we bought the farm, my folks moved away, and we moved back to the farm. Now it's my turn.

Sixth time:

My wife went back to college (CMU) to get her nursing degree. So, I watched two little girls under the age of four, two nights a week. We had four rows of cows for the girls to ride their tricycles behind. It was about forty-five feet to carry milk from the cows to the milk house, dump the milk into the bulk tank, and return. Thirty seconds max! What could happen? In about five seconds, Lori ran her tricycle into the gutter, tipped it over, and crawled out of the gutter on her hands and knees. (No, the cows didn't kick her, but they could have.)

So I hauled her to the milk house, turned the spray hose on warm, and hosed her down. My wife got home from college and wanted to know why Lori was wet. I just said she was playing with the hose in the milk house. (I did let her spray herself.)

Seventh time:

My wife was off to college, and I was watching them. They were playing in the sandbox under the tree. I had to use the bathroom. They will be fine. Just as I was leaving the bathroom, the phone rang. It was the neighbor's wife. She said our two little girls had come

144

to talk, so she gave them milk and cookies. She thought we might want to know where they were. Lori had walked her sister an eighth of a mile, and got cookies to boot. She had just turned four years old.

Eighth time:

Farmers know that you can bale dry hay until the dew comes. It was a dry dark June night, and I was still bailing hay onto the ground. My tractor had no lights, so I was doing the best I could in the dark. I always watched the hay being picked up entering the bailer. It was very easy to keep the tractor next to the row. So, watch the bailer, not the tractor.

Periodically I would look down the window of hay. What is that white thing moving in front of the tractor? I hit the clutch and brake at the same time. I was about 1,000 feet east of my house in the dark. It was Lori waving at me. I was sad, happy, and mad all at the same time. I shut down everything, picked up Lori, and headed for the house. Lori had done it again! She and her sister had been put to bed, checked on, and they were both asleep. Mom went to sleep in the chair. Lori woke up, came downstairs, unlocked the back door, and walked more that 1,000 feet all alone across a field toward the sound of daddy's tractor.

Ninth Time:

We had cousins visit from California. A farm was a new experience for their family. After lunch we grown-ups were having coffee. All the kids were excused and playing in the house. The visiting mother jumped to her feet, simultaneously saying, "Oh!" My wife asked, "What's the matter?"

"Your daughter just pinched my boob."

Lori, surprised somewhat by the reaction, said, "Daddy does that to mommy all the time."

Of course, I'm taking the fifth.

Tenth time:

Lori and her sister were being watched by Gramps and Gram. The grandparents had a fuel oil tank (250 gallons) in the basement. It was filled through an exposed pipe outside the house. The deliveryman put 200 gallons in by putting his fuel hose in the pipe. After he left, Lori put Gramps's water hose in the pipe and flooded everything. He carried out over 250 gallons, 5 gallons at a time, of worthless fuel.

When I presented Lori with this list of her accomplishments on Easter day, she said, "You missed one, dad." Lori and Grandma had a secret.

Eleventh Time;

Grandma was a spic and span housekeeper, and on one of Lori's visits Grandma was down on her hands and knees scrubbing the kitchen floor with a bright yellow hand brush. Lori went to the refrigerator, picked out a bright yellow, full pound of unwrapped butter, went to the living room carpet, got down on her hands and knees, and proceeded to clean Grandma's carpet floor. The yellow butter brush covered much before it was gone.

After this story was related to me, I realized Lori's walk in the night to my tractor was not my daughter's first near-death experience.

All the precious short stories covered about thirteen months, ending at 4 years 3 months of age. Good Lord, what were we to do with this kid? Then it hit me, problem solved – send her to school early.

This marvelous person is now a professor with a PhD at a state university. She still does everything, but it's for everyone else. I thought about sending this to her university to see if Lori had it all correct on her resume.

P.S. The good Lord blessed me and humbled me at the same time with this child.

Grand Marshall

My Sunshine has done and accomplished many things for one lifetime and is not done yet. Her time as a high school custodian did much to broaden her horizon on people. Her way of reuniting run-a-muck kids, loose in the hall, with their non-concerned parents watching the basketball game was cool. Showing boys how to open a bathroom door without injuring the person entering the room. Finding out how the new teacher wants the room situated so she only needs to teach, not rearrange. Everyone had a first name, even the superintendent. That's only what she used or wanted to be called by.

Apologized immediately for her mistakes. For example, the first time she cleaned the teacher's lounge she threw out the terrible pot of coffee, only to find out it was a special blend of the principal. Later on she informed the principal that his great coffee was regular coffee beans burned and sold at a high price and Yuppies like him buy it. His response was, "Really?"

She replied, "Yes," and walked out.

As time passed the high schoolers grew very comfortable with seeing her every afternoon. Many kids confided in her, shared their life experiences with her. Many questions came from high school girls about boys. They didn't dare to ask their parents. Sunshine tried to advise for the welfare of the student.

As time progressed, more questions, many times. Her wisdom was cherished. Then the question she didn't have an answer for. Two senior girls representing their class asked, "Jeannette, would you please be our Grand Marshall in our homecoming parade?"

School friend advised, do not turn that down. So she agreed to be one of two Grand Marshalls, with Mrs. K., the principal.

Sunshine

You have heard the phrase, "He is a man's man." There is also a wonderful phrase, "She is a woman's woman." A heart of gold. A mind of steel. Plus a will to conquer any obstacle. I have two sunshines; one that happens every morning and one beautiful person that makes my day all day, every day, "Sunshine," my wife.

I think she has many reasons to be P.O. at life. But she isn't.

Sunshine is a cancer survivor. On her second pacemaker. Experienced heart failure. One child is on total disability because of a car-truck head on wreck. Ten days later, her daughter became 80% paralyzed because of a rare disease called Transverse Myelitis. She was put on total disability immediately. One year later she lost a step-daughter to a rare liver disease. Next her other son had a motorcycle accident. Was air lifted. Did survive. Some memory loss and deaf in one ear.

So you see Sunshine has been thoroughly challenged. Her go to phrase is, "Well, I'm not dying today." So the following is just one of the many things she does for people.

Eight years ago she decided to have a week long "Woman's Week" and birthday party. So she started planning and collecting for up to 15 guests. Enough beds were found, over 20 identical chairs were located. Her daughter had four tables. For over three years she searched and found a 30 place setting of special dishes with all the serving dishes. Note: the silverware used all that week was from "Surf Powder Detergent" her mother collected in the 50s. Sunshine had catered for over 27 years so all cooking pans were covered.

The Woman's Week

It happened 5 years ago. The following is what she planned and how it happened.

Rules "none" just fun!

1. Age 7 – 70 years.
2. Attendance: come as often as possible or all week.
3. Come and go as you wish.

4. Bring anything you wish to share. (The ladies did furnish many things to share.)
5. Your favorite food – no limit.
6. No guest will cook, clean or do dishes.
7. The best part: The ladies did what they wanted, when they wanted, any time all week.
8. Relax! It's woman's week.

The following is what she planned and the ideas the women furnished. All women slept in one big room in her building. They could turn off the lights and talk until they fell to sleep or watch a movie on a six ft. screen.

They slept as long as wished to. No alarm. Anyone could get up early to watch the sun rise or watch the sun set, relaxing on the deck. Some chose to stay on the deck after dark and talk, but most often they just sat quietly and listed to the sounds of the night.

Comfort Food

Food on request. Eat when you're hungry. Each lady's favorite food was served at least once. (They brought it or it was made for them.) Sunshine's oldest son provided a homemade red raspberry wine treat. It was excellent. Sunshine made a beautiful cake for the Saturday birthday party.

The lake and golf course named in honor of her mother, "Louise." A canvas tote bag was given to each guest with" Lake Louise" embroidered on it plus small presents.

One Rule

No men allowed, only to cook, clean up or whatever the women asked to be done.

To start the week, each guest held up a picture frame and got their picture taken behind it.

Indoor Events

Listen to music, play card games, do puzzles, or rest. Read, read poetry to others, laugh a lot, play board games, talk. One thing extra good, one person brought a play and everyone played a part. Plus Sunshine took them to her store, and they got to dress for their part. (much fun.) They all had and answered questions like:

1. What was the best thing that ever happened to you? Note: No man made the cut!
2. What was your favorite movie and why?
3. What is your favorite thing to do?
4. What would you change if you could?
5. Different day, different questions.

They also did henna tattoos. The 7 year old gave foot rubs.

Outdoors

Sunshine even arranged for a limo if the women wanted or needed to go anywhere. (It was free, as was the whole week.)

Let's Play

1. They played golf on her golf course and had golf starter lessons for free if desired. (Some did.)
2. One of the lady's very favorite things (which they did many times) was playing croquet
3. barefooted on the golf green. (It gives you a fuzzy, good- feeling foot massage) very relaxing.
4. Played volleyball same way. More exercise, less fun.
5. Had horseshoes to play or toss a Frisbee.
6. Go swimming or fishing in Lake Louise.
7. If wished, could paddleboat around the lake and listen to the frogs.
8. Many, many pontoon rides every day on the lake. Running quietly or listening to the pontoon radio.
9. A perk: cell phones don't work well here, so no calls in, also no one called out.
10. A big A-framed wooden swing to relax on and swing under the shade tree.
11. One night her son put up an outdoor movie screen at the lake, showed a movie and served popcorn and pop.

12. There was a campfire every night at the lake. Once, margaritas were served. Ladies choice.
13. There are two tracks on Sunshine's 80 acres so the guests took frequent long walks in the woods, talking and smelling the flowers.
14. The handicapped lady rode in a golf cart, any where, any time. It had lights and a horn.
15. The city gals got to see many birds and animals very often.
16. On the day that the most people (27) were able to come, Sunshine had a picnic on her stone built golf tee – hamburgers, hot dogs and the strawberry wine, if desired.
17. Many times that week I sat on our house deck and enjoyed their laughter. It was great!
18. One brought and launched sky balloons.
19. Once they watched a chipmunk steal the cat food. Chipmunks don't eat it all at once. They fill their cheeks over full and leave looking like they have the mumps.
20. The evening before the birthday party itself, her son, who is handicapped, and a great cook, put on an outdoor fish fry with all the trimmings. Mm, mmm!

Sunshine catered the Saturday birthday party. Some of the ladies came from as far as Banden,

Oregon, and Everett, Washington or as close as Blanchard, Michigan.

Sunshine's week was a great success. I asked what she liked best about the week. Her answer was "Everyone really enjoyed themselves."

She still is giving and doing for people every day.

I think the best thing she ever did was "asking me to marry her."

Surprise Birthday Party

"Are you available to cater a birthday party, date given?" "Yes I am."

Location established. "Are you able to decorate and cover all things?"

"Yes," price agreed.

My wife had catered many, many events for years. Everything being ready to go, she was set. One of her kids called, "Mom, I'm stranded come pick me up."

She had time. "I'll be right there."

Upon returning to the party site, in her absence, a large sign was put up. "Happy birthday, Mom!"

She had just catered her own birthday party!

(Yes, her kids paid the bills.)

$50 Deal

The results of long marriage render many tender, loving, fun and memorable memories. Some will be the couples only; some will be shared for the benefit of others. The marriage bond is solidified when each person is totally comfortable with what's shared. After a hiatus of 10 years between marriages I tried again at age 59. This lady was occupied with something 24/7. I thought it might be interesting to interject a speed bump in her schedule.

So I implemented the $50 deal. This lady is a true business woman. Grandma has a secret and I won't tell."

My Perfect Job
1. No background check required.
2. Working condition: fabulous
3. Union rules permanent.
4. My authority unquestioned.
5. Wisdom and job knowledge expanded daily.
6. Job security was never in question.
7. My money management skills were needed constantly.
8. Never wanted or needed time off.
9. Continuous daily perks.
10. Bonus pay was unbelievable.
11. My art collection fills a room.
12. I still get dividends every day.

13.   I loved my production program coordinator. She was fantastic. What she produced was perfect!

Oh, what's my job? Being a Dad!

Why Life is Great

A warm hand in the night. The wordless message. A single tear on her cheek means happy. The phrase, "Take your time, I'll wait."

"You'll never guess what happened!"

"I'm pregnant."

Silence says everything.

You don't have to tell her, she knows. What a wonderful thought! It's impossible to describe *together*. Two singles, back to back, makes a home run!

A solid wall makes the best family circle. Life is the car, family is the engine, friends are the scenery, have a great trip.

A statement describing a life done right: when you're born, you cry, the world is happy. When you die, and the world cries, you should be happy.

The Limo

Flint Online Auction: For Sale – Limo, white, good tires, all leather seats, telephone from front to back, stereo music, electric partition between driver and passengers, tinted windows. Stepson made one low bid; he got it. Let the good times roll. Granddaughter first to ride, plus me. Her dad drove home. She giggled and said, "It's fun to be rich, gramps." (Six years old.)

First use: Her birthday party. Son dressed in a dad's shirt and hat. Picked up her guests and took them to" Chuckie Cheese" and then took them home in the limo.

Second use: We all were able to ride in it to many Mother's Day dinners. Funny, people were impressed with limo riding folks. We received many business cards. I got one card giver. I told him we weren't very rich. We only owned half of Lower Michigan and just one of the Great Lakes!

Third Use: The limo was used for Women's Week travel.

Fourth Use: Daddy-daughter Dance was a big hit.

Fifth Use: He dressed and limo-ed all the proms his son attended.

Step-son did a bucket list request with the limo. The Elvis Presley impersonator agreed to being picked up by limo onto McBride to chauffeur a terminal elderly person around the area, while she got to visit with her hero's impersonator. It was an extra great day all around. Stepson said her smile alone paid for the whole trip.

Sixth use: My stepson coaches many baseball teams. Not all of the boys could get to the area ball field to practice. So he just hauled them all in the limo. No one missed practice after that.

Seventh use: If you go to the casino by limo, automatic special parking.

Eighth use: We were all set to limo to a golf tournament, but it was rained out. My golf friends would have loved it. I was very disappointed.

He did many good, charitable and fun things with the car. Finally, it was put up for sale. Four college boys purchased it. They were trying to decide who would drive it first. My stepson solved the problem. "What is your favorite beer?" he asked.

One beer named was my stepson's favorite. So that guy drove first.

First Daughter Married Second

First daughter married second at St. Charles Catholic Church, Greenville, Michigan. No, I didn't pick the church. But I didn't object, either.

As the wedding reception progressed, the normal clinking of glasses to have newlyweds stand up and kiss occurred, very often, in fact. Well into the event our bride needed to leave the room. Seeing she was gone, the kissing clinking started up loudly. Our groom played his part well. Stood up, looked for his bride, put his palms up, shrugged his shoulders, and presented a sad face.

My second daughter, realizing there are many duties to being the maid of honor, sprang to her feet, walked directly to our animated groom, grabbed him, kissed him and clapped her hands all the way back to her chair. The crowd's reaction was super loud, but got ever louder as our bride re-entered the room.

Daughters were always there for each other, no matter what was needed or price to pay. My daughters and the boys are the same way.

I Was There, I'm Lucky

The best best man speech ever: My grandson entertained many ladies before his choice was finalized. His first of two best men stepped to the mike. "Pete, one last thing I want to do for you before your married life really begins. Emily, please put your left hand on the table."

She did. "Pete, please place your right hand on top of hers."

He did. "Enjoy the moment, Pete, because that will be the last time you ever have the upper hand."

*　　*　　*　　*　　*

A once in a lifetime memory: my oldest stepson's second marriage, his new wife's first. Exit after vows was not the regular walk with music. She wore a white dress and red shoes. They "Skipped to My Lou" up the church aisle to polka music. What a way to start life together!

*   *   *   *   *

My second marriage my best man was a woman, cousin Anne. Much surprised, but very happy to do it. "Do I have to wear a suit?"

After our Greenville ceremony and reception we left for Mt. Pleasant, Michigan (long trip.) We stopped at Walmart to leave our film of the event. Entering the store in our suit and wedding dress we were noticed. The photo lady stating the obvious, "Just married?"

My new wife's answer, "We're actually honeymooning. First stop, we went to Walmart!"

For middle-aged people's honeymoons, Walmart is the "to go" place."

P.S. My bride wore her daughter's wedding dress when we married, a reverse of tradition. And I wore my son's suit.

Marriage

Being married 31 years the first time, I took 10 years off for good behavior, before I entered the sacred halls of matrimony a second time. There was much discussion about do's and don'ts. What's tolerable and what isn't. After all was settled, we married. She is definitely a woman of her word. No surprises, but there was a special add on: "Remember, Chuck, I don't *need* you in my life, I *want* you in my life!"

I pondered the statement and sometimes I would ask for clarification. The reply: "You will figure it out."

The solution came to me early one morning. "I had to give up." She told me.

"You're not needed for what you can do, but you're wanted because of what you are!

Bucket List

Would you please join me as I relive my one and only visit with Santa?

"How did you get by security?"

"I told them I was looking for my grandkids."

"Aren't you a little old to sit on my knee?"

"There is a little kid in all of us, at any age, besides your knee is hard, and it hurts my back!"

"Really, how old are you?"

"I'm 78, Santa, my clock is ticking. It's now or never; let's do this! Please look at my list."

"We stopped making most of this stuff 50 years ago. Besides, you will only get up to three presents from me."

"What do you mean, three presents?"

"Do I need to remind you that my step-kids hunt, and can shoot reindeer?"

"Gramps, you have a Harley on your list, you are too old!"

"No, I'm not. Look Santa, it's only three equal payments of $12,259.99 each."

"What I want the most for Xmas is just one HOLE IN ONE, Santa. I would get down on my knees and beg, but you would have to help me up."

"Sorry, Gramps, but I can't do miracles."

"Well, thank you, Santa, for the visit. I can take this off my bucket list. It was great!"

"You're welcome, Gramps. Oh, is your mother picking you up?"

"Maybe."

Dedicated to Shirley Pool
Kevin is No Ordinary Man

The saddest time of my life and a highlight in my life are both in the following story.

Late on a Wednesday afternoon in 2006 I received a call from my son-in-law stating that my daughter's liver was failing and we all needed to be with her at Detroit's Ford Hospital. We all made it by 7:30. She was still in the E.R. We talked with her. Later that night she was moved to the top floor intensive care unit! We stayed in the hospital's apartments.

Early the next morning, we all went to the top floor waiting room, and took turns visiting her. All day long and into the evening one man was there all the time. He was about 6'4" tall, well built, 250 pounds, well dressed, black man. We talked. He said his name was Kevin. I told him why I was there. He said that he was there for his brother. I couldn't sleep. So about 2:00 a.m., I went back to the hospital to see her. Kevin was sitting alone in the dark waiting room. When I left he was still there.

When I arrived Friday morning, Kevin was there. He was there all day. That afternoon, my daughter was put on life support. She was not able to talk to us anymore.

I went to sit with her around 3:00 a.m. Saturday. Kevin was in the dark waiting room, all alone. Next time I went by the waiting room, Kevin was gone. My son-in-law and grandkids were in there talking. It was soon decided by all that the machine was to be shut off. We gathered around her bed. My youngest grandchild walked up to his mom, not really understanding totally what was about to happen, and told her he loved her. I had to leave the room.

I walked down the hall to a windowsill, sat down, and cried. I looked up and there was Kevin. I said, "She's gone."

He sat down beside me, hugged me, and said, "I know, but I want you to know I picked up a young man this morning, and I'm here to pick up your daughter. I want you to know that she is safe and very happy."
He hugged me again and walked away. I never saw him again.

It took me a while but I'm very sure that Kevin was not an ordinary man. I felt better. What do you think?

****

My mom outlived my dad by twenty-nine years. After her memorial service I was tired and sad. I went to bed early. I lay in bed thinking, "Do you suppose mom and dad are together? In heaven?"

For some reason I said out loud, "Kevin, are they in Heaven together?"

I did go to sleep finally. I had a strange dream.

I dreamt that I awoke from sleeping on my mother's couch. I looked at my mother's room. There was a very bright light all around her bedroom door. I got up and opened the door. The very bright light was in the form of a ball near the ceiling. The bedroom was completely empty – no furniture, no clothes in the closet, and all her pictures were gone. The room's light started to dim. I noticed night was changing to day.

I looked out the west bedroom window. The sun was coming up fast. (Why was the sun coming up in the west?) Then I noticed a very old, old car coming down the road from the west. I left the bedroom and went to the front porch. As I stood in the porch doorway the old car went slowly by. My dad, as a young man, was driving. The young lady beside him was my mom. They were laughing and enjoying themselves. I waved at them but they didn't look at me. I felt happy.

Then I woke up and I thanked Kevin for his answer.

I have no explanations for why these two things happened but I'm very thankful for Kevin.

I would like to dedicate the true-life stories you just read to my friend, mentor and editor, Shirley Pool. She talked me into writing humor, about school bus driving, and my trip around the word. She always made it better. And if you are lucky to know of Shirley and Nile, they both made everything better. They are both on my special people list with Kevin. They all made my life better.

Thanks Again

Monday, 12:35 p.m., just pared hole seven, leaving the green my cell phone rang, "Chuck here."

It was my stepson. I was expecting his call. I asked, "Are you playing Sunday?"

"Yes," he answered, "but not why I'm calling. I found mom laying in the grass, unconscious. Called '911.' First responder came, revived her somewhat. Now she is on her way to Mid-Michigan Hospital in Mt. Pleasant by ambulance."

"Where is Mid-Michigan Hospital?"

"Right behind Applebee's on M-20."

My golf-mates golf-carted me the full length of Links of Edmore course to my truck and I was off cross-country to Mt. Pleasant.

So much goes through your mind: Second pacemaker. Doctor said she was terminal. Please, Kevin, let me say 'Good-bye.'

M-20 was bad traffic: slow and very frustrating. As I approached the first light of Mt. Pleasant, my phone rang. Stepson said, "She is doing better."

I got to the hospital. Sitting in the E.R. with her, I was impressed by the thoroughness and bedside manner of the male R.N. As the nurse, busy at his work, came close to me, I knew my guardian angel was with us. The R.N.'s nametag said, "Kevin."

Three hours later, Sunshine left the hospital, diagnosed with a negative reaction to new medicine. They sent her to a cardiologist.

Looking at Her

As I sit here writing something for the paper, I look at my Sunshine sitting in her chair. It's great just to look at her. I don't listen well, so I put everything into looking. I know I'll always want to keep looking at her.

Oh, it's starting to rain, but I can still see Sunshine. When I say "my Sunshine" it does not mean I own her. It means I understand that she agreed to share her life with me!

The invisible bond between us won't be broken because she created it and maintains it.

There is one hundred and fifty four years of memories in these two chairs. You younger folks wonder what there is left near the end of a long relationship. It's like the end of a long, long rope. There is a knot, or in our case, a bond, that ties everything together. The bigger the bond or knot, the easier it is to hang on to. I hope you all have a strong grip!

Little Things I'm Thankful For
1. A firm handshake.
2. A warm smile.
3. Happy kids.
4. Phone call from 2,200 miles away, "How are you?"
5. Honesty: no worry!
6. A rainbow: a good ending.
7. The cardinal in the snow.
8. Our cat scratching on the window.

9. A bald eagle circling up high.
10. Woodpecker at work.
11. Rain changing a yellow cornfield to green.
12. "I love you dad," good any time.
13. "Need help with that?"
14. That I learned early my way wasn't the only way.
15. "I agree, you're right!" Tranquility.
16. The correct answer isn't always the best answer.
17. All my spankings were earned!
18. I learned much more from a "No!" than from a "Yes!"
19. "Hi neighbor!" means many things.
20. The other side of the hill is easier!
21. "Looks good, doesn't it?" Success!
22. There is enough for everyone!

To Hear Just Once More

To hear just once more again:
1. Daddy! Daddy!
2. Can we play ball?
3. Do you like my sand castle?
4. Oh, please, dad!
5. Why not?
6. Can we keep him, Dad?
7. What's a worm?

8. Do I have to?

9. Can I pet him?

10.   They're so cute!

11.   Well, dad, it's this way."

12.   That's fun, can we do it again?

13.   I don't understand, dad!

14.   I'm glad you're my dad!

15.   Why are boys so stupid?

16.   I don't understand girls!

17.   Why does a farm smell?

18.   Daddy, how can a tractor run without legs?

19.   Is there a doggy heaven?

20.   Why doesn't a caterpillar have a tail?

21.   It's my turn! It's my turn!

22.   Why are there rules!

23.   "Yes," is a happy word. "No" isn't.

24.   Hey, dad, you just got promoted to Grand-dad!

A Forever Christmas Present

This incident happened after Christmas two years ago, but proves beyond a doubt that giving and sharing is good any time and no amount of money can cover it.

My grandson is autistic. In his senior year, he was made manager of the basketball team. The Tri-County coach had him suit up for the last basketball game against Fremont High School. Andrew was sent in to play the last 1-1/2 minutes of the game. Almost immediately, he was fouled?? He made one of two free shots.

Fremont then inbounded the ball. Their player totally missed the toss in?? Andrew caught it and made a dog shot. Fremont possession again, down the floor and scored. Tri-County inbounded the ball. Andrew was left alone in 3-point territory??
His shot missed. Fremont rebounded the ball.

Their player threw it to Andrew. He made that 3-pointer. A total of 6 points in a minute! It wasn't that he scored 6 points in one minute, which was great, what was important is that he was given the opportunity to try!!

I thank the two high school coaches and the nine wonderful young "men" that made it happen.

This is an example of year 'round Christmas spirit at work and play. I hope the "one minute" will be remembered and cherished by those who made it happen, as it is for my grandson!
When you give of yourself, you're refueling your spirit!

Merry Christmas to you all.

A grateful grand-dad, Chuck Houghton.

The New Year's Eve Blizzard of 1976

Thirty inches of snow was predicted for the evening; we got it. The Lints, Giffords and Houghtons were invited to the Binkleys at Hall's Lake for cards and lunch. Normal travel was out. After a few phone calls, it was decided that Don and I would drive our John Deere tractors with heated cabs, pick up the Lints and attend Binkley's New Years Eve party.

Talk about "close friends!" Try putting six grown ups in two tractor cabs. It was fun. About 2 a.m., after a great time, we headed for home. The snow was up to the axle on the front of our tractors. We dropped off Lonnie and Naomi. At Blanchard, Don and Janet went east, Jeanette and I went west. Somewhere between Blanchard and home, a big pickup started following in my tractor tracks, the only other survivor of the night I'd seen. The truck stopped at Rick Walkinton's.

The nine and a half miles from Hall's Lake to Chuckette Farms was nerve-racking. I was relieved when we made the tool shed. We waded the deep snow to our back door. Made it. I reached into my pocket for my house key. The key was in the car. We drove the tractor, so we were locked out. Another "Chuck It" Farm memory.

Happy New Year!

Notes

Politically Speaking

I don't like either political party. We as American are allowed to criticize: a local restaurant and tavern owner has only one rule: No talking politics in this building. The following chapter I'm trying to be a poor substitute for Mark Twain as I poke fun at politics.

Thinking About Politics

I was thinking the other day, and as my wife would say, "That thought is scary all by itself!"

Anyway, I was thinking America has bad political problems since it was created. I look at all the people who couldn't vote over that period: Indians, Negros, women and immigrants. The list goes on. One group has never been disenfranchised in our country's history: white males. We have more women than men. It is possible we could lose our right to vote, for say, 20 years. Just think, men, where we will be if things improve in that 20 years. My wife doesn't think this is scary at all.

We are actually a very small group considering everything. Add in all the groups we oppressed. If it was an amendment to the constitution, even the Supreme Court couldn't save us.

*   *   *   *

I never write about politics, but one thing is constant when politics are discussed at senior centers. Political parties are running and ruining America. I don't think very many men from either party could survive an open book of their life. I don't think religion should get into politics. They pray to open a session, but we can't pray in schools. Women don't count much to either party; please look up the process a woman needs to go through to charge a congressman with any sexual wrongdoing.

The constant bickering wastes 90% of the time used. There are more woman than men in America so I propose the following: a national vote. Only women can hold any Federal elected office.

My reasoning for this: who is in charge of the home and family?

You got it! If women went by men's rules, they could take over America.

*   *   *   *

I find election years quite expensive and unhealthy. The political ads are so muddy I had to invest in new knee boots. I switched the ads off and on so much, I have blisters on both thumbs and one finger is infected. I had to buy a dozen batteries for the TV remote.

Of course, we viewers know all along that all negative ads regarding the opposite party candidates have to be totally false because neither party would be foolish enough to support a poorly qualified candidate. I would find it very hard to spend my money for a negative ad. It would be like buying something I didn't want. Isn't it a shame when it is as beneficial to pay for a negative as for a positive? What kills me is everything is "Fake" news, so what are political ads?

The Primary

The best way to primary vote is on page 12 of the Lakeview Area News, August 2, 2018 issue. There is a list of all people running for an office in our primary, with each person's party listed, along with the words, "Choice of one."

The highest Republican, Democratic, Libertarian, one from each party would be on the regular ballot. I would vote for people from each party. But I have to pick one party. I just lost my right to choose. No party has a monopoly on quality people and never will. Both gerrymandering and party line voting should be removed from politics.

"Now."

I always wondered how on your SOAPBOX mixed with elections. Soap is clean. Campaigns are not. Soap Boxes are slippery. I had to install handrails in mine.

Religion and Politics

Need a war to improve your economy? Religion or politics are historically proven to work as reasons. The two are so close in make up and completely compatible.

1. Both words have eight letters.
2. Both groups follow a leader blindly.
3. Neither allow for change.

4. Our way is always right and our tests prove it.
5. Compromise shows weakness.
6. There are thousands of religions and all countries have numerous political parties, so one isn't special over the rest.
7. Look how harsh each is if you don't agree or conform. Only they can judge.
8. Neither have any faults.
9. If something didn't work, not our fault.
10. Both use the other to obtain goals.
11. Neither can admit to any damage done.
12. Each survives because of money.
13. You can buy your way into both anytime.
14. Religion and politics will protect you from the "law."
15. They both prove that we are not created equal.

How to Fix Government
1. All donations for all state and federal offices would be received by a state, non-political licensing bureau.
2. No one can receive private donations.
3. Everyone would receive the same amount of money to run for office. Out of state money would be shared equally.
4. All donations would be public information.
5. No party line voting period, neither primary nor general election.

6. Anyone can run for office, but must register with licensing bureau to do so, plus nomination petitions.
7. All people vying for a specific office would be listed in the same column with a R-D-I after their name. (Vote for one.) The highest vote received from each party would be on the general election ballot. Highest vote wins.
8. Time limit on campaigning of 3 months total.
9. All left-over election money be used for wounded vets or national debt. No elected official leaving office can receive any retirement or insurance except president and vice-president.
10. Instead of free money to other countries, pay off student loans. Straight flat tax, no exceptions on income tax, stock, or perks, same as cash.
11. If you are receiving government support and use tobacco, you will be required to do extra work, or receive less pay.
12. No retirement acreage set aside for tobacco payments.

Fun with Politics
1. Laws are great as long as Congress isn't affected.
2. Politics are like cards. If we have Trump we'll be in the game.

3. I wonder what would happen if Congress "never" got paid for each day the government was shut down.
4. The only requirement needed to hold office is being able to give a 5-minute answer to a "yes" or "no" question and not answer.
5. We have so many contaminated politicians in Washington the CDC- AMA had to vaccinate.
6. Most politicians are lawyers. It's very apparent none have read the book, "First Kill All the Lawyers."
7. You're not rich until you own at least two politicians. Personally I would rather own one than be one.
8. Remember a politician will stand for what he thinks people will fall for (Mark Twain).
9. We have so many politicians being canned or expelled our unemployment rate is gong up.
10. I loved this one. I find much humor in "No congressman qualifies to be on the House Intelligence Committee."
11. All politics are 90% one party griping about the other. If they got paid for what they accomplished Congress would starve.
12. I just watched my first political campaign ad on TV for 2018. I didn't get halfway through it. I went to our mudroom and check my boots for leaks.

13. As Mark Twain stated, "To run for office can be a very rewarding endeavor, especially financially."
14. Well it's an election year, and if you are a TV watcher I send my sympathy. I always thought if I could invent something that automatically turned off TV commercials I would be rich.
15. I have never voted straight-line party ticket. I feel way too many people paid too big a price for me to party-line vote. I owe them the respect that I voted for the best person.
16. One more: my cousin and I were golfing and talking about party-line voting when he pulled a Mark Twain on me. He said, "I have a relative who is a totally party-line voter. He would even vote for Lassie if the dog was on the ballot."

P.S. It's very hard to tell when Congress is not in session; results from Washington remain very constant.

The first baby was born to a lady senator in history. It's our only proof that the political process was reversed at least once.

Just For Fun

Political parties do so much for my **well-being**. They are the only pain that comes with an off and on switch. Any communication device fills the bill. We will never rid ourselves of political parties because that is the only thing they agree on: that parties are absolutely necessary.

Once a week the news media should publish or report on T.V. what Congress or state legislators have <u>done together</u> for our well-being. Wait change that to once a month. Otherwise some weeks, there would be no report.

It's been years since I've heard a "yes" or "no" answer from a politician. I bet I wouldn't get a "yes" or "no" answer to this question, "Mr. or Mrs. Politician, would you give me a "yes" or "no" answer to a "yes" or "no" question?"

"Maybe." Both parties are always right. What's wrong with that? Poking fun aside, folks do you think loyalty to party is affecting the welfare of our country?

I do.

Oh Well

I think sometimes as we age "Oh well" covers up too much stuff. We can laugh even if we can hardly move. When you see a cat chasing its tail. Funny, yes, but I have seen people do that. More fun in watching a hummingbird fight. They are very territorial. Can you imagine a disagreement over anything as big as a thimble? The magnitude of most arguments can be covered by a hill of beans. I'm beginning to think all our elected people in Washington are reincarnated hummingbirds. Or maybe tree frogs, which blend in anywhere, do nothing, but make a lot of noise.

I would love to be paid for doing nothing. I'm so good at it I would get a Christmas bonus. I don't think we have to settle for "Oh well" much longer. Automation will save us. We already have people-less cars and I would invent a robot lobbyist. (I'm very sure the president would finance me.) Which could easily convince Congress it could do all of their mundane work.

A law would be passed immediately and unanimously by both houses to fund the robot, not realizing the ramification of what they did. Their workload went to zero and they just put themselves out of a job. But they all would go out in a blaze of glory, blaming the other party all the way home. (On their own money, of course, the robot wouldn't pay for clean up.)

"Oh well," I had a dream. Relax, the nightmare still exists.

Political Satire

We are going to make America great again, but not the way our current president thinks. We killed off the Indians and stole their land. Our first census we had over 670,000 slaves. The Chinese built our railroads. We chastised the Irish. We imprisoned the Japanese. The Mexicans harvested our crops. The list is endless. The reason our country was and is great is because all of these nationalities' citizens survived and are still with us. Mr. Trump is going to prove America is truly great, yet we will still be the same people even if he is president for eight years. I thank you, sir, for the ultimate test. We will survive even you.

Differences

The differences in people are man created, not by the natural progression of man. We all laugh, cry, think, love, create, share. But to me we all are equal because we all bleed red. Some people are taught to hate, so when these people bleed white blood, they might be able to declare superiority. Until then, we are all the same.

Soap Box

I rarely get on my soap box and because of O.S.H.A. I had to install handrails just to do it now.

I wish the top three people of each party would sit down by themselves and list their goals for each and every American and for America as a whole. (Not how to do it!) Then have the two parties compare lists. I bet the results would be almost identical. The problem is each party wants all the credit for getting there, their way.

Is this a true statement?

The only group of Americans who were never restricted from voting is white males. So if this is a true statement, now, as a group we are definitely a minority. So what do you think will happen when we run out of money? The door is open, ladies. Vote!

Notes

Dementia

Tell Them Now

The evening of February 13, my phone rang. "Hello."

"Dad, are you all right?"

"Yes, Chris, I'm setting in my chair."

"Are you sure you're okay?"

"Yes, why?"

"Because yesterday was my birthday."

"Oh, son, I'm so sorry, I forgot."

I missed my son's special day. Dementia again.

I thought back to when my dad was in the hospital for a seemingly minor problem. We talked and shared for a long time. As I was leaving I stopped at the foot of his bed and said, "I love you Dad. See you in the morning."

He didn't make morning. I got lucky and was so glad I told him. From that experience I have adopted the philosophy "If it's good, tell them now."

So maybe the missed birthday was a wake up call. I decided I needed to tell my kids and step kids face to face, one on one, that I love each and every one of them. I'm very proud of the people they are and how terrific my grandkids are. I finished my goal with my daughter on Easter Sunday. Thank goodness because around 6:30 p.m. April 2, I had my fourth stroke. I'm not a ghost writer, so I survived again.

If something you feel needs to be done, "Do it now." Pay anyone a deserved compliment. Put yourself out for someone. Wouldn't it be great to start an epidemic of kindness? Pick a day. "Oh, today is open."

Why Not?

Dementia doesn't always make sense. The mind jumps from one thing to another, or is it necessarily believable. Why did I do that? You got me? So as you read this chapter, pleas hop skip and forget along with me. I'm trying to give you a lesson in Dementia: "Okay, what now?"

This side of nothing.

"Well," he said, "Write a book about dementia."

Easier said than done. I wrote about 732 pages on the subject, but I don't remember where I put them.

The other day, I was playing cards. I jumped to my feet and yelled, "Euchre!"

The fellow to my right said, "Sit down. You do that when you play Bingo."

I was playing Euchre with three ladies. The lady to my left had dementia. So a fourth lady was helping her play. I had shorts on. Something was running up my left leg. I looked and started to laugh. My card partner wanted to know why. I answered, pointing to my left, "She is playing with my leg."

All three looked and laughed. She didn't stop playing with my leg. I stopped laughing long enough to say, "I guess I still got it."

More laughter. All five of us were laughing. Dementia changes your libido.

The Best Thing About Parkinson's

My doctor just told me I have Parkinson's. I find it interesting, as I get older and keep slowing down, the only things I can still catch are diseases. The following comments are what I think of having both Parkinson's and Dementia:

1. You can't walk far enough to get lost.
2. Bugs will get dizzy and fall off you.
3. You'll be surprised how evenly you dispense salt and pepper.
4. Hope you don't lose your voice because when people ask to hug you, your head will be saying "No."
5. With Parkinson's you hear things. Don't worry, with Dementia you'll forget anyway.
6. No dust will ever collect on you.
7. No problems; it's easy to shake things off.
8. People give you more room when they see you coming.

9. When you're out in winter, people will think you're just cold.

10. Parkinson's can be added to the list of things you can't control.

11. I would be a great bartender.

12. People won't know if they're making you nervous or not.

13. Can you imagine the reaction you would get, entering an operating room dressed appropriately and announcing, "I'm your surgeon?"

14. I would starve in China – I can't thread a needle.

15. I don't need a hand to shake; I already got one shaking.

16. When asked "Give up?" I would never answer with my head.

17. I'm an honorary member of a religious group, the Shakers.

18. With Parkinson's I could never pass the police sobriety test walk.

19. A hand-writing expert would never identify me.

20. My arms become tired holding hands.

21.　　If you're a control freak, Parkinson's will drive you nuts.

22.　　I was never much good at doing two things at once. Now with Parkinson's and Dementia I can shake and forget at the same time.

23.　　You'll never guess how much money I have saved on people trying to sell me items.

24.　　I don't buy anything at auctions either.

25.　　I have to be very careful when Sunshine asks for help, I answer verbally.

26.　　And no, young man, you don't get Parkinson's from too much dating!

27.　　I think I stopped thinking?

The Best Thing About Dementia

When you're old, you forget what you are missing. You might spend 10 minutes looking for your hat, then you find it on your head. It's possible to check if you locked your house 4 or 5 times, but you only remember the one time you remember that you locked it.

I will squint my eyes and try very hard to think of something. Usually the only result is I would pass gas. If you have had brain injury, your chance of dementia is much higher. I had two. Can't remember your car?

Push the button and the vehicle with the lights blinking and horn blowing is most likely yours.

Three things or statements I will never forget:
1. Yes Dear!
2. Yes Dear! And
3. Yes Dear!

With dementia you're not expected to pick up items from the store. Birthdays, anniversaries and money – missed them all. Not picking up your mother-in-law (may be forgiven.)

Wife to husband, "You didn't pay me yesterday."

Husband, "I don't know."

On the golf course, "How many strokes?"

"Four."

"You weren't even on in four."

Two golfers with dementia, "John, what is your ball name and number?"

"Round and white."

"Same as mine, Hmm."

"Yep."

"Pick one."

One golfer kept count of his swings with balls on a string but he didn't move the ball all the time.

You will never need to identify someone and if you have dementia it won't matter anyway.

People with dementia have problems with numbers. Have help available for all business deals, regular driving close to home is good. Trips to strange locations – not good. When driving just drive, do nothing else, period.

Sometimes with dementia your personality can change: be happier, be quieter, etc. You won't necessarily forget everything all the time. Mom was 99 when she broke her hip. I visited her each day. About two days before she was to leave rehab I noticed she had her shoes on wrong. "Mom, are you having my mind problems?"

She said, "No, the nurse put my shoes on that way."

If you have something in mind, if interrupted you might forget it all. You are always in the moment, but you're 5 minutes late. I need to talk out loud to even count to 100, which is hard to do. You can get very religious with dementia. You go to a room, "What am I hereafter?"

What you do on a regular basis you're good. What you do rarely you must re-learn.

You can afford to be an avid reader. Buy one book, read it over and over. It will always be new and interesting unless it's funny.

*   *   *   *

Dementia is assisted by bad bumps on the head. I had two. The first, age about 13, one Farmall wouldn't start. It was a very cold winter day. Dad hooked the log chain to one of the three cultivator bolts on the BN Farmall, the other end to the C to pull start the B.N. Being cold, I had on one of those old felt Deer hunting hats. The B.N. started to start, jumped forward, making slack in the log chain, then died. Chain strained, bolt broke, chain end hit me in the head. The hat saved me. But I had a spot of gray hair above my left ear about the size of a dime until all my hair turned gray to match.

The second bump, the boys and I were working on the big upstairs barn doors. The steel track came down and hit me on the head.

This Side of Nothing

Having read many books, sometimes a big word will come floating out of me. I play cards in a Euchre league. As we play we talk. I used a big word. A fun-loving friend and fellow player stopped playing, looked at me in his special way and said, "Do you even know what the hell that words means?"

"Yes, if you remember the word, you remember its meaning. It all helps friend, it's your deal!"

(P.S. I did tell him what it meant. I need to go over and over things many times to be put to memory even that doesn't always work.)

And sometimes, was that a fact or did I dream it up? I'm glad to have notebooks I check. You have to buy an extra pair of shoes because you are always retracing your steps.

If you're lucky when you are going around in circles you'll stop and go the other direction so you won't get dizzy. Have fun with dementia. I tell my kids it's your turn to watch me. You lucked out. There were two of us watching four of you! It's eight of you watching one of me. You will probably have to call in the grandkids. If I see or hear something nice someone does for or says about a person, anything, I can get instantly emotional.

Can drive with dementia. There is no reason to listen to instructions. One is too many; have them written down. When you have asked someone the same question more than three times, expect a different answer. Sometimes it's just a look.

I can't fix my dementia, so I just smile all the time. People think I'm thinking good thoughts and I can't tell either way. I find I can remember jokes but not ideas. Anything that creates humor is good because some people with dementia are very ornery. I remember Ben at the senior center. He could get from home to the center, played a good game of Euchre and got back home. Nothing else registered. I wore my nametag upside down playing Euchre, but that's just for me.

I love to mow lawn because you always know where you're at (that's a good feeling.) And it's always good to accomplish something. Strange sharp noises go straight through you. It hurts your head so stay off the cat's tail. So some people with dementia are happy and some are mad. Sounds like normal people, doesn't it?

I used to know what a person was thinking, now you hear yourself say, "What? What? Start over."

I brought an elderly gentleman home once from a "Home." He hit some golf balls and we took him fishing on our lake and he caught many fish. (He didn't remember doing it, but was happy for a week.)
I told my step-son, "Please don't stop teasing me, even if I don't know you."

His answer, "Should be easier, I won't have to call you by name."

Never change doctors because you can't answer the 100 questions you'll be asked. It isn't what you remember, it's what you can't forget.

My friend's mother was in a Home in Mt. Pleasant. They visited mom regularly. She didn't know who they were, but she always wanted to go home. It's where we feel safe. My wife's aunt in a home got her coat on every day and said her husband was coming to pick her up. Before she went to the home we took her to her church supper. She picked up the plate of food, didn't like its look, so she dumped it on the counter. She forgot how to change her mind.

If you show something to someone with dementia, and they seem happy, keep showing them.

They won't remember how often. Do you know what you call two people with dementia? I forgot, tell me!

If all ladies forgot how to change their mind, just think how many things wouldn't have to be rebuilt, redone, returned, removed, the list goes on.

Oh yes, it would be the same for men.

You can't read fast to dementia people. They can't follow the words. Out of sight, out of mind. With dementia the mind does not know what it's looking at. The Statler Brothers song, "Counting Flowers on the Wall" means much more now than it used to. Dreams are so off the wall with dementia. I will put in every odd dream I have from now on.

Here is an example: A friend of mine shared this; he also has sleep apnea which means you sleep with a mask strapped to your head covering your nose and mouth.

He dreamed an octopus had him head on with its tentacles wrapped around his head and was suffocating him. Being a very strong man he was able to tear the octopus off his face. (He could have whipped two men and picked his teeth at the same time.) He woke up to find he had ruined much of his air equipment.

As I have said, people with dementia do drive quite well. But I think there should be a list of phone numbers conveniently obvious to anyone outside your car looking in.

*   *   *   *

I'm sure that my dementia is hard for my personal family members to accept. So I try extra hard to not make any situations worse. It's very hard not to be impatient. "So what?" is a good phrase to live by. My family and step kids are coming around to "Let's have fun with dad."

I know it's hard on my wife because it's 24/7 for her. My last dream was (remember I said I have crazy dreams) my wife was complaining about the 24/7 deal, which she never does complain about anything. When she said (in my dream) I have got you all the time. The kids only show up when their car breaks down at the end of our road. My wife is "mother hen'ing me; must be I'm still a good egg!!

There are some advantages to dementia. I ride my stationary bike once every day. I get it done and go about whatever I'm doing. After a while, "Oh, I forgot to ride my bike," so I go ride it. So on occasions I have taken my once a day ride two or three times.

If anything goes wrong or gets broken you will get the blame. You won't remember if you did it or not. Grin and bear it.

Memory and medicine don't mix. Thank heaven for daily pillboxes, but eye drops for glaucoma is a challenge. I do eye drops three times a day. So I line up the bottles back to front on my nightstand. As I do each treatment I put the bottle next to my air machine. As I go often to the bathroom, I have to look at the nightstand. If it's past a treatment time and the bottle is still out I immediately do the treatment and put the bottle in its "I done it location." They were calling numbers as they picked team members for the Monday morning golf scramble at the Links of Edmore. Number 15 was called twice, then I called it. No answer. I looked at my number. It was me. I had forgotten in 2 minutes.

As you can see from reading this part how my mind functions some times.

I'm going to stop all this and write a book!

Inspiration

What I write about jiggles my brain around 5 a.m. many mornings, maybe because of my lifetime occupation. Farming started every day at that hour and my mind is ready to go, even though the rest of me isn't. I don't know why, or for what reason it hits me, but if I don't get up and make notes, my dementia will take over, and it's all lost. I start to tell Sunshine something. She shushes me to hear the TV. I will forget what I wanted to say. But I'm beginning to think there is a positive side to this. My five o'clock memory gives me something that happened 40 – 50 – 60 years ago,. The best part of all of this is it's all good fun stuff. I find it interesting it is only good memories, why not a negative event?

My second inspiration is a location, not a time. The bathroom. Why here? I keep a note pad in the room and don't ask. Actually I do have time to analyze this provocative question, but I feel the restraint of confinement, which won't allow for a broad overview of the subject. Oops! I'm sorry! I listen to too many political ads. Answer: none, it all went down the drain.

Oh yes, I'm going to write a book.

The Reward

A full life is hardly a day in time. I had my day, here it is on one page. What really counts, all summed up.

Man, this is a dark lonely path. "Oops!" I fell, got my hands dirty. Be careful; try not to stumble again. A warm hand in mine; it's not so dark now.

Four little lights in a row. I can see more of the world. The four lights are becoming higher and brighter. The path is smoother and easier to walk. No longer do I see or feel the warm hand.

What's this? A second warm hand and three more lights along the way. Path being much wider and brighter is good!! Everything is comfortable and rewarding! "Oh no!! One of the seven lights just went out!"

It's raining on the path. How can one hurt so much? But I must thank heaven for all that the light illuminated while it still shone. The path has changed to a steep uphill grade. But it's easier walking, because now I have 39 lights of all sizes and shapes to help and show me the way.

The man tending the gate just said, "The entrance committee voted 5 to 5 on your admittance."

But he ruled, "You tried hard and your word was good, so come on in, sit down, make yourself at home. It's never dark here."

Then the smile. "Your daughter is waiting, first room on the right."

Kids and Grand kids

I have no way to express anywhere near how much you all have blessed my life. I talk to Teri often. When my time comes, I promise you now, anytime you want to talk, I will be listening.

Love,

Dad

I've been a dad for 59 years, a dairy farmer for 37 years, a school bus driver for 17 years, a semi-truck driver for 5 years, wrote articles for the paper for over a year, and author (when the books were delivered) for one day.

I enjoyed life, family, people, baseball, bowling, slow-pitch softball and golf. having kids, kids having kids, grand-kids having kids,

Both of my wives were named Jeannette. I sleep much better because the name is the same. I've been around the world, but as a school bus driver, I've been able to see the world as a child sees it. That is beautiful, And I count my blessings.

For more copies of this book

www.amazon.com/Chuckle-Chuck-Houghton/dp/1790443334

41213479R00123